Moon Flyers

Best wishes,
Barbara V. Papes

Moon Flyers

A FAMILY MEMOIR: COPING WITH MENTAL ILLNESS

✣

Barbara V. Paper

Copyright 2015 by Barbara V. Paper

All rights reserved. This book, or parts thereof, may not be reproduced in any form or by any electronic or mechanical means without permission in writing from the author, except by a reviewer who may quote brief passages in review.

ISBN: 1507699417
ISBN 13: 9781507699416

Printed in the United States of America

In Memory of Pinny

Preface

There is a difference between occasional depression and mental illness. Depression is an imbalance of chemicals in the brain. Having mental illness is not something of which to be ashamed. Telling a family member or professional about symptoms is not a character flaw. A person cannot just snap out of it. The result could be suicide or early death resulting from complications.

During the late thirteenth century, the word lunatic came into use regarding those whose behaviors were foolish and eccentric. The term expanded to mean crazy or insane. The origin of the words lunatic and lunacy have their roots in the word luna, meaning moon. Many people believed such unusual behaviors were dependent upon the changes or phases of the moon. Other negative terms came into the modern vernacular that also attach a stigma to the meaning of mental illness. Some of these are bonkers, cuckoo, daffy, loony, screwy, and wacko. In 2012, the Congress of the United States passed a bill that all federal laws would no longer use the word lunatic. President Obama signed the bill and it is now the law.

Even though I do not proclaim special expertise regarding mental health, I am going to share some of the information I have gleaned during my research for the book. Primary sources are the Mayo Clinic, Dr. James Messina, Rabbi Carl Perkins, National Alliance on Mental Illness, and Marsha M. Lineham.

One mental health association, confirmed by the Mayo Clinic, reports that 3-4 million men show clinical signs of depression. The risk increases as men get older. An estimated 40 percent of men will suffer some degree of depression between the ages of 40 and 60. The number of people who were diagnosed and treated is much smaller. Other behaviors that often manifest themselves in depressed men are substance abuse, lack of discipline, inappropriate rage, and irritability/anger—considered masculine attributes, not always recognized for what they represent.

Self-medicating is a term used in the story. Rabbi Carl Perkins of Temple Aliyah in Needham, MA, wrote in an article regarding alcoholism ". . . In every age, men and women have succumbed to the deleterious effects of alcohol and other drugs. Alcohol has long been known to humankind as a source of comfort in times of stress. For example, in the biblical book of Proverbs 31:6 we read, 'Give strong drink to the hapless and wine to the embittered. Let them drink . . . And put their troubles out of mind.' "

This is not a textbook. However, I describe an illness originally considered under the umbrella of bipolar conditions, now identified as a separate mental disorder known as **borderline personality disorder.** I learned that many mental health professionals still do not recognize this condition in some patients. There are therapists and psychiatrists who hesitate to accept patients with BPD because of the challenge of successful treatment, even though it is listed in the 2013 edition of the *Diagnostic* *and Statistical Manual of Mental Disorders,* a manual for mental health professionals. The mental health resources listed at the end of the book are good examples of the numerous organizations, support groups, and online references available to anyone who wishes to learn more or find help.

Thanks to the National Alliance on Mental Illness (NAMI) and other reputable sources, I found there are a number of criteria for diagnosing borderline personality disorder. A patient does not necessarily exhibit every behavior. Some of these are:

- frantic efforts to avoid real or imagined abandonment
- a pattern of unstable and intense interpersonal relationships; destroying a good relationship just when it is clear that the relationship could last
- a pattern of undermining themselves at a moment when a goal is about to be realized
- identity disturbance: markedly and persistently unstable self-image or sense of self
- impulsivity in at least two areas that are potentially self-damaging: spending, sex, or substance abuse
- reckless driving, binge eating, and shoplifting
- recurrent suicidal behavior, gestures, or threats, and self-mutilating behavior
- chronic feelings of emptiness
- inappropriate, intense anger, or difficulty controlling anger

Other associated problems:
- bipolar disorder causing mood swings and eating disorders, such as bulimia

- post-traumatic stress disorder (PTSD), experienced by returning Iraq veterans
- attention-deficit/hyperactivity disorder (ADHD)

I have read that BPD is diagnosed predominantly (about 75 percent) in females. About 2 percent of the general population suffer from this illness. It is also pertinent that BPD is about five times more common among first-degree biological relatives, as with father/daughter. Additionally, there is an increased risk for these individuals to suffer from substance abuse and other mood disorders.

Dialectical Behavior Therapy is a system of therapy to treat people with borderline personality disorder, originally developed by Marsha M. Linehan, a professor of psychology at the University of Washington. DBT combines techniques for emotion regulation with concepts of distress tolerance, acceptance, and mindful awareness largely derived from Buddhist meditative practice. DBT may be the first therapy experimentally demonstrated to be generally effective in treating BPD. While the research on DBT was initially conducted with women diagnosed with borderline personality disorder, DBT treats women who binge eat, teenagers who are depressed and suicidal, and older clients who become depressed frequently.

Throughout this book are examples of personality traits described by James J. Messina, PhD, who is a licensed counselor and teacher in Tampa, FL. He writes, "**Codependent personalities** evolve from an irrational attempt to keep some type of order in a hurtful relationship. A codependent spouse makes excuses and lies for the addict." It is so easy to be caught up in the trap of destructive behavior. Dr. Messina lists some of these codependent behaviors:

- low self-esteem
- sense of personal insecurity
- inability to take risks
- fear of failure
- inability to forgive and forget
- compulsive behavior e.g. perfectionist, meticulous, inflexible

He says that the fear of rejection is the "act of giving to others more power than I give to myself over how I feel about myself." He also writes that, "Fear of rejection is the driving force behind many people that keeps them from being authentic human beings. They are so driven by the need for acceptance of others that they lose their own identity in the process. A depressed individual or mentally ill person also can exhibit this fear. What the others say or feel about me is the determinant of how I feel about myself. I am completely at the mercy of others for how happy or sad I will be. My self-satisfaction and belief in myself is in their hands. Fear of rejection is the abdication of power and control over my own life."

Acknowledgements

I am not certain of whom Mr. George Ade, American writer, was referring when he explained that he had decided to write for posterity after being turned down by numerous publishers. Although many publishing houses have rejected my manuscript, my goal is to write for posterity as well and for all who seek to learn about a world of individuals who quietly lead lives of unspoken sadness and stress.

My good friend, Chaim Charyn, devoted time and special insights to help me complete the manuscript. I shall always be grateful for and honored by his friendship. I appreciate Amy Boulware, Jewish Federation of Greater Chattanooga Social Services Director, and Ann Treadwell, Program/Development Director, who have been supportive and helpful with their suggestions.

How can I not give credit to my family? My sister-in-law, Jacqueline (Jackie) Paper Weissman, allowed me to share her family's background and write of her mother, father, and brother, whom she dearly loved. My children, who endured so much during the difficult years, make my efforts worthwhile. There is no way I can express just how much they mean to me.

My appreciation also extends to the members of the North Georgia Writers Group for their talents and helpful critiques that have been invaluable. I enjoy meeting with them twice each month.

Although I know it's unfair, I reveal myself one mask at a time.

> Stephen Dunn
> Poet

I have an uneasy feeling around—aversion to—anyone wearing a mask. The young and young at heart chuckle when they see a masked clown and enjoy the fun of scary Halloween masks. In certain countries, as in older times, actors wear masks in plays to identify characters; the masking art of Japanese Kabuki Theater comes to mind. Nonetheless, masks frighten me. I cannot see the person behind the mask. Is there a smile on the face or a frown? Is this person kind or cruel, happy or sad? I can't tell.

We all wear masks at some time in our lives. We conceal our authentic selves behind forced or insincere smiles. We hide our inner feelings when we stifle anger or tears in reaction to a hurtful situation—putting on a straight face. We often appear to be what we are not.

During my lifetime, I have worn different masks. At times, my mask was that of a contented mother taking my children to music lessons and participating in their activities, so no one would see my underlying concern for overwhelming problems.

As a wife, my smiles hid the turmoil I experienced in my marriage. My stoic professional countenance disguised the strain of the stressful reality of my life, over which I knew I had minimal control.

One day I decided to write two short stories regarding memorable events in my life. My plan was to submit them for magazine publication. I shared these stories with a friend, who encouraged me to expand them into a book. Once I began, the words flowed. I felt compelled to write about my husband, Paul, and all that he suffered, with the intent to give direction to others who similarly suffer and hope to the people who love them. Paul bequeathed two very special gifts—whether he knew it or not—a sense of humor and the power of determination. I was uncertain if I should be so forthcoming, or if my children would approve.

It did not take long before it became evident that this is not just Paul's story; it is also that of our older daughter, Hara. It is through her eyes and courageous struggles that I finally began to understand what happened to my husband. I realized I must toss my masks aside and feel free to express the unspoken words that I held tightly inside for so many years, mental illness. I wanted the words to be written boldly and spoken with a forceful voice.

Each writing session was a catharsis for me. There were days sitting at my computer, when tears flowed. After many years of introspection and numerous revisions, I completed *Moon Flyers*. The story chronicles the lives of two individuals who responded to mental illness in two distinct ways. Throughout the creative process, it occurred to me that being able to see humor in often stressful life situations, retold in the original short stories, helped me cope and survive. There was more for me to achieve than just completing a book. With the support, encouragement, and the expertise of the staff of the Jewish Community Federation of Greater Chattanooga, I have spearheaded a number of mental health programs for the Jewish and general communities. I hope to continue these programs in the future. The following are stories of two of my loved ones who met their challenges with two different outcomes. If *Moon Flyers* provides lessons for others as they struggle with their own lives, then I am gratified.

Parting is all we know of heaven,
and all we need of hell.

Emily Dickinson
Poet

DALLAS, TEXAS

Paul, a certified public accountant, intended to work at his office the second weekend of October in 1986 to complete his clients' income tax extensions for the Monday deadline. With Paul away from the house, my father and I decided to visit family in Dallas. I will never forget Paul's words as he sat next to me on the edge of our bed. He looked downward at first and then slowly raised his head, his eyes directed toward my eyes. "I have ruined your life," he told me. Never have I seen anyone look more defeated. It broke my heart to watch the man he had become. "Paul, you haven't ruined my life. However, you know we do have to talk about finances when I return."

The last words I ever heard from my teary-eyed husband were, "I know. Have a good time."

It had been a bittersweet weekend in Dallas. Aunt Louise, my late mother's younger sister, took Dad and me to a stage show on Saturday evening, featuring music and dance from the fifties and sixties. I immediately thought, I wish Paul could see this. He would love it. My aunt and I had a great relationship. I felt comfortable enough with her to discuss Paul's current behavior. Because my dad was staying at my cousin's house, Aunt Louise and I were alone at her dining table having breakfast. During her visit to Mobile the previous year, she had seen the change for herself.

"Things are really bad at home."
"With Paul?"
"Uh-huh."
Tears started to make their way down my cheeks.
"Aunt Louise, do you remember when you were visiting us for Rosh HaShanah (Jewish New Year)? We went to my temple for services and Paul came later than we did."
"Barbara, was Paul drunk?"
"He acted like he had been drinking."

I reminded her that I was concerned Paul would make a scene. He was speaking in an atypically loud manner, as if he weren't in a house of worship. That's why I got up from my seat and met him in the foyer.

"Paul, have you been drinking?"
"Do you want me to leave?"
"Yes. I do."

I don't know if anyone saw that he turned around and left. I returned to my seat as fast as I could. Paul had never before gone to worship in that condition. I couldn't believe that he would do something like that and didn't know that he drank in the morning. He could have been drinking at his office. I never would have known.

"Aunt Louise, I hope you understood. It was so embarrassing."
"I'm so sorry, Honey."
"I honestly don't know what I am going to do."
"I know it's hard. Is there anything I can do to help?"
"I wish there were. Just being able to talk to you helps."

MOBILE, ALABAMA

I had left my car at the airport. When my dad and I drove home the following Sunday morning, I saw the paramedic's vehicle pulling away from the front of my house. I knew Paul was in the ambulance. I later learned that Bobby, Paul's friend and client, had gained access to our house when Paul did not come to his office for a prearranged meeting that morning. According to Bobby, the two had spent the previous Friday night out drinking and socializing when Paul said, "I don't feel good. I'm going home." The next day, Saturday, Bobby told me that he dropped by Paul's office to check on him.

"Paul, you look terrible. What's wrong?"
"I didn't sleep all night. I feel like shit and it's hard to breathe."
"I think I should take you to the hospital."
"No, I don't need that. I'll go home."
"Paul, at least get something to help you breathe."

After much insistence from Bobby, Paul went into a pharmacy to purchase medication. Bobby followed in his car and watched Paul as he came out with a package. He left Paul at that point. "Bobby, then what happened?" I wanted to know.

"When he didn't show up for our Sunday morning appointment, I got worried and went to your house. It wasn't like Paul to miss a meeting without letting me know."

"How did you get in?"

"I went to your next door neighbor for help. She had your emergency house key."

"Yes, I forgot."

"Barbara, I found Paul in bed. He had his hands raised above his head on the pillow; he looked just like he was sleeping."

Bobby discovered Paul too late to save him. Later I found an unopened bronchial inhaler on our bedside nightstand. That was probably what he had purchased Saturday night. It seemed Paul had just stopped breathing during the night; perhaps sleep apnea was the ultimate cause. His death certificate listed heart and circulation problems, but many factors led to that moment. Paul had let his health go unattended for a long time.

The next few days were a blend of stress, pain, and grief. There was so much to think about, and it was so difficult to focus on the funeral I had to plan. I considered asking to see Paul's body for a final farewell. I couldn't. I wanted to remember him alive, even though that recollection was terribly painful. I had to arrange for our daughters to come from their respective college campuses, notify the newspaper, and contact family and friends. There I lay, alone in bed, trying hard to sleep. Troubling thoughts were racing through my mind. What am I going to do? Will I be able to support the girls in college? How am I going to manage?

I did not sleep well for many nights to come. In 1986 the U.S. Space Shuttle Challenger exploded and disintegrated upon liftoff. That's how I felt about my current situation.

I arranged a graveside ceremony, an acceptable Jewish custom. As my family and I were driven through the Spring Hill Avenue Temple Cemetery gates to the gravesite, I recalled the same trip two years earlier to bury my mother. Her passing had been the first time I had experienced the death of someone close to me. I wonder if this is the same limousine we rode in last time. Everything seems familiar, except then Paul was with the girls and me. I returned to thoughts of my husband who was soon to be placed in the ground. Why can't I cry? I feel numb. I recall saying to my daughters, "Your dad is no longer in pain. I hope he is finally at peace." There wasn't any more to say than that.

The mass of men lead lives of quiet desperation.

Henry David Thoreau
Writer/journalist

MOBILE, ALABAMA

The day was clear in Mobile during late October 1986, soon after Paul's death. I drove down the familiar tree-canopied Government Street and parked my car near the brick building on the corner as I had so casually done for many years before. I noticed there wasn't as much Spanish moss hanging from the ancient oaks as I recalled from my childhood and wondered if it was due to air pollution. However, there were more pressing issues on my mind this time. I entered through the rear door, dreading the task ahead. The elevator made its way to the third floor, opening to allow me to exit to my late husband's office directly across the hall. It was time to remove his personal possessions and what remained of his assortment of green plants, so that another accountant could occupy the space. My husband normally was fastidious in his personal appearance and in maintaining his office, except for his oversized desktop, which he told me he organized for his work, but looked to me like an utter mess each time I visited.

When I walked into the room, I couldn't believe my eyes. His business retreat, which housed his accounting papers, books, clocks, and wooden animal collection, was abandoned, unkempt, and dirty. I found moldy food in the small refrigerator by his desk. Each of the formerly lush potted greeneries housed on the glass window shelves was wilted or already dead. This did not look like the accounting office I saw the year before when I helped him meet tax deadlines. I boxed some of our personal papers and his collectibles. I was checking all over the office for items to take home when I made an unexpected shocking discovery.

Behind the curtains was a small rifle. What was the gun doing there? Paul was never a hunter. He had a strong aversion to guns and joined me in forbidding any weapons in our home. In his filing cabinet, I found a box of bullets. Then I remembered.

During the previous year, Paul told me, "I tried to kill myself, but couldn't do it." At the time, I was somehow relieved and encouraged that he wanted to stay with us. My current discovery revealed that he probably was inept with the gun. He just did not know how to do it or was too afraid. The reason does not matter now. What will I do with the weapon? I felt fairly certain Paul did not have a license; I certainly did not intend to handle it, even though my father had taught me how to shoot when I was a young girl. The accountant who shared the office agreed to get rid of it for me. I never asked what happened to the gun; I didn't want to know. Why would a man with a wife and two daughters who loved him bring himself to the point of wanting to end his life?

Further examination of his file cabinet revealed an assortment of *Playboy* and *Penthouse* magazines. My goodness, I had no idea he had these! I never saw any type of girlie magazines at home. I sat down in his oversized desk chair with tears in my eyes. A gun, bullets, sex magazines, and dead or dying plants; these could not be my husband's legacy.

Wine comes in at the mouth and love comes in at the eye; that's all we shall know for truth before we grow old and die.

>William Butler Yeats
>Poet

Tuscaloosa, Alabama

Who was the man I married? How did a true Southern belle meet a boy from the Lower East Side of New York City?

The year was 1957. It was an ordinary wintry late afternoon during my sophomore year at the University of Alabama in Tuscaloosa. I decided to spend some time away from the Delta Phi Epsilon sorority house where I lived. I walked several blocks to the Student Union, a building that housed the campus post office, supply store, radio station, and snack shop. My destination was the snack shop, the SUP (soop) Store in the college vernacular. In no hurry, I strolled past some buildings to the corner brick building on a path that took me down the stairs and to the right. It was quiet. Few students were there, not unusual for midweek. Passing the food counter on my left, I found a corner seat and table on the far side of the dining area to spread my papers without attracting too much attention. I enjoyed the change of scenery to catch up on some of my assignments and finish a few letters. My favorite stationery, woven rice paper with an Asian design, was in the pile. As I was beginning to write a letter, I spied a tall, heavyset young man out of the corner of my eye. He ambled up to the table.

"Hi. That's unusual stationery. I'm Paul Paper."

"Hello. The stationery was a gift from my uncle. He sent it from Japan. My name is Barbara Vogel. Do you want to sit down?"

I don't recall seeing him before that evening, though I later learned that Paul was a member of Alpha Epsilon Pi, the same fraternity of other young men whom I had been dating—maybe he had noticed me at some party. Perhaps I did not pay enough attention to the fraternity freshmen; I was a sophomore at the time. Paul and I talked for a while.

"May I walk you back to your house?"

"Sure."

We conversed as we walked. Then Paul suddenly stopped.

"There's a Military Ball on Friday night and two fraternity parties on Saturday. Will you go with me?"

"Yes, I'll go."

His spontaneous invitation surprised me; we had just met. I don't know why I immediately agreed. Yet, there was something about him that made me feel comfortable. He was older, obviously intelligent, and seemed more mature than the college boys I already knew. We spent several more hours in the sorority television room immersed in deep conversation, neither of us knowing what television programs we were missing. I wondered about the plans for our first date. Before Paul left, I questioned him.

"How can you get into a military dance?"

"I am an Air Force veteran. I was able to get tickets."

Foster Auditorium was the campus basketball stadium and event center. It was not an elegant location, even though the dance was formal. Most of the men were in military dress uniform. Paul wore a nice looking dark blue suit. I wanted to look special for the evening, so I wore an emerald green cocktail dress, a sheath with a detachable green net overskirt with matching shoes, an outfit my mom and I had seen at a fashion show in Mobile. After that show, I convinced my mother that I had to have that dress.

Paul was a terrific dancer, very light on his feet for a large man over six feet tall, weighing at least 200 pounds. When we danced, we seemed to fit together. Normally he had a full head of black curly hair. I had to wait to rediscover this feature because his head was now shorn almost bald as part of the fraternity ritual of initiation. Although the bowling ball look made his shoulders seem broader, I didn't mind, and it certainly didn't bother him. Perhaps it was true that opposites attract; we really had little in common. Nonetheless, we both had a great time that night and at the following day's events at his fraternity house.

The family you come from isn't as important as the family you're going to have.

Ring Lardner
Writer/journalist

NEW YORK, NEW YORK

Paul's family provided a loving environment to overcome the struggle of life in New York City's Lower East Side. I know little about his forebears, not even certainty of their native countries, except that his family name was originally Papier. Paul was born in 1932 and given the Hebrew name Pincus in honor of his late grandfather, Pincus Cherkes. Pinny was the family nickname for him. Pincus was one of the high priests mentioned in Scripture, grandson of Aaron the High Priest and a flawed individual, according to commentaries I have read. From all I learned from his mother and sister, Pinny was a loving, dutiful son and brother. His sister, Jackie, gave me some of his school autograph books, popular at the time in New York. Looking through them, I learned that his sixth grade public school class named him most cheerful. Paul was considered the best dresser according to his autograph book from Junior High School 188.

Paul confided some of the early stresses that helped shape his personality. The family's financial struggles weighed heavily on him.

"Barbara, we had a very small apartment. My sister and I shared a bedroom. I slept in the top bunk and tried to give her as much privacy as I could. In one of our apartments our bathtub was in the kitchen." I never had heard of such an apartment layout. The concept was strange to me.

"My family did not always live in an apartment," he continued. "We had a nice house." When his dad, Harry, was drafted into the Navy during World War II, circumstances drastically changed and a family move was necessary. During those years, Paul's mother, Lillian, had to work two jobs to make ends meet. These were difficult times for her and her two young children. She knitted and crocheted clothes for them. They were always well dressed and well fed, but compared to the other Paper relatives, Paul was quite aware of what they didn't have. His father's health deteriorated upon his return from the service, limiting Harry's ability to work.

I asked Paul about his childhood. "We liked to play stick ball," he told me. "I sometimes would sit on the fire escape balcony when it was hot." I related to that. Summers in steamy Mobile could be brutal. My dad moved my bed to the nearest window during the hot months to enjoy a rare summer breeze. Paul and I grew up in the time before most homes had air-conditioning.

Paul said he had an IQ score of 130 when he was tested; this, I never doubted. "School was so boring. Sometimes I would read a book during class. One teacher always thought I wasn't paying attention; but I knew the answers when she called on me," Paul said.

He occasionally acted out from boredom. A teacher who liked and encouraged him, Mrs. Quattlander, took him under her wing. With her assistance, he applied for entrance and eventually attended Stuyvesant High School for gifted students. Yet, he never graduated.

This was the first of his pattern of retreats when life presented what he perceived to be overwhelming challenges and stress. It was not the scholastic challenge that deterred him. Paul said, "My family didn't have much money. I wanted to be a doctor. There was never going to be money for me to do that, so, I just left school." He was very discouraged. I have no idea whether his parents knew about his dream. I don't think Paul ever applied for scholarships. Perhaps scholarships were not so available during those times; I just don't know. I do know from what he said that depression at this early age caused him to leave school around the age of sixteen.

The National Alliance on Mental Illness (NAMI) reports that over fifty percent of students with a mental disorder, age fourteen and over, drop out of high school. That is the highest dropout rate of any disability group. "I worked a number of menial jobs." Paul once worked for the Streit's Matzah Company. As he put it, "I worked in the farfel mines. I didn't know what I wanted to do. So, my friend Sam and I decided to join the military."

Mobile, Alabama

In contrast to Paul's background, I can trace my fraternal forebears back to the 1800s in Alabama where my paternal great-great-grandfather built a home now listed on the historic homes registry of Mobile and currently houses the Mobile Carnival

Museum. Around the same time, my mother's parents, Samuel and Jennie Spitzberg, started a life in Little Rock, Arkansas.

I was in the same elementary school for eight years. Junior high (or middle) schools did not exist in Mobile until a number of years later. I filled my high school years with study, youth activities, and many parties. During the 1950s, the United States was involved in the Korean Conflict and there was official fear of a nuclear invasion from the Soviet Union. Some frightened Americans built and stocked underground bomb shelters.

Mobile was the site of a military supply base and not far from other military bases in Pensacola, Florida and Biloxi, Mississippi. Our high school had evacuation drills. One drill had all students and teachers boarding buses and driving at least thirty miles outside of Mobile in case of a nuclear attack. I have no idea why anyone thought that taking us out of city limits would be any kind of protection. If an attack came, I'm not certain what we would have done next. There would have been hundreds of high school students in buses, with no additional instructions. At the time, I thought that was a ridiculous waste of time. I never felt fearful, nor did any of my friends.

*See one promontory,
one mountain, one sea, one river, and see all.*

> Socrates
> Writer/playwright

Tuscaloosa, Alabama

Paul told me more about his background. U.S. Air Force assignments in medical supply took Paul to Europe and finally, to Clovis, New Mexico. Paul loved those four years of life, and particularly enjoyed touring around Europe when he had a furlough. The Netherlands gave him the most pleasure. He told me, "I never learned to speak German, but all I needed to know to get through Germany was the phrase Ein kleines Rhine wine, Fraulein." (A small Rhine wine, Miss.)

Paul knew there was an expansive green world beyond the confines of Central Park and the miles of cement and high-rise buildings of his former world.

"I really liked New Mexico."

"Why?"

"I learned to ride a horse."

"Really? Where did you ride?"

"Well, there was a lot of open space in Clovis."

From time to time, a man with a pony would go through my neighborhood in Mobile offering short rides. I have a photo of myself on a pony, taken when I was around seven or eight years old. I have never been on a horse.

After serving his country for four years, Paul was granted an honorable discharge from the Air Force in 1956. He never had considered going to college, though he achieved a G.E.D. diploma. Lacking the courage and self-assurance to apply, Paul allowed his military friend, Sam, to apply for him. Sam had confidence in Paul who just signed the necessary admission papers and requests for additional funds for his education through the United States G.I. Bill. Before he knew it, it was 1957; Paul was at the University of Alabama, pledging a fraternity. This was another new life for him. I told Paul that Sam sat next to me in my freshman English class at the university. I did not know him well; we spoke very little. The irony was that Sam never returned to college the semester when Paul arrived. We never saw or heard from Sam again, though he had helped redirect Paul's life.

Paul was a good student, enrolled in the Business College, working toward a career in accounting. I was amazed that he was able to pass college level algebra without ever taking the subject in high school. Many classes were rather easy for him; he was a quick reader and remembered everything he read.

My future husband was a many talented individual. Before we met, he had tried amateur boxing. He showed me a photo taken during one of his matches. He gave up this sport because of his poor eyesight that began when he was a child. Without his glasses, he told me, "I had trouble seeing my opponents." However, he loved to play Ping-Pong and won an inter-fraternity tournament in college. The university newspaper dubbed him *The Ping-Pong King.*

I do not know why he often struck a pose showing off his biceps and sucking in his tummy, like a Mr. Universe contestant. All of the pictures looked funny to me.

Give all to love; obey thy heart.

Ralph Waldo Emerson
Poet/essayist

From the beginning, Paul was determined to win my approval. Unfortunately, he was so insecure at first that I did not receive a letter, a postcard, or telephone call from him the entire summer after we met. I was not impressed. School began again the following fall; Paul decided that he had made a terrible mistake by not contacting me. He was right. Before class registration began was sorority rush week when prospective new members were entertained and chosen. I spent most of my time rehearsing for the skits we presented. Often Paul came by the sorority house to see me; I deliberately paid little attention to him, though I saw him out of the corner of my eye. Anyway, I was too busy kicking, prancing, singing, and trying to remember my lines.

I fell extremely ill during that week with a severe case of the Asian flu. Three of my sick sorority sisters and I were ordered by our sorority president to go to the University Infirmary. "You do not have a choice," she told us. "You must leave the house now."

The infirmary was an unimpressive brick building. The sterile interior was not particularly appealing. The semi-private bedrooms were typical of the hospitals of the 1950s, metal bed frames, one dresser, no decoration, and a window with a view of nowhere. It was extremely quiet in the infirmary. The nurse stuck thermometers in our mouths and showed us the rooms where we were to spend the next week. The doctors did not realize just how volatile this little virus would become and allowed visitors during the week of our confinement.

To my surprise, Paul appeared at my bedside with a selection of magazines for me to enjoy. There I lay, looking pale with no makeup on my face and feeling awful. So what did Paul say to me?

"Barbara, I'm sorry I did not contact you this summer. I really didn't know what to write."

Paul paused.

"Please go steady with me."

"You can't be serious. I'm not going steady with you. We hardly know each other."

This was my second glimpse of Paul's impulsive nature. I informed him that another boy whom I had been dating brought me candy. The candy really had nothing to do with my decision. The comment seemed like a good comeback for this situation. I was surprised and didn't know what to think or say to Paul, even though he flattered me by his invitation. A campus epidemic of the Asian flu followed. The hospital released us at the end of the week to provide beds for new patients, even though I truly did not feel ready to return to my usual activities. So many students became ill; by the time the doctor discharged us, beds were lined up in the hallways.

Paul persistently pursued me for months after my hospital release. One evening I was studying for an exam in the sorority house dining room. Paul came in. I had not expected to see him. He sat down across from me, looked at me and asked, "Will you please go steady with me?" After a few thoughtful moments, I relented and told him, "Yes, I will." He was interesting, very romantic, and funny. This time I decided I had nothing to lose by giving him a chance. He gave me a fraternity necklace to signify that we were going steady.

One should never despair too soon.

> Frederick the Great
> King of Prussia

It was an ordinary weekday night during my junior year. I studied for a while at my sorority house before Paul came over. Paul had scraped up the funds to buy a used car to get around campus and for our dates. I bought new tires. A blanket served as upholstery for the front seats. He usually took me out for a hamburger and drink. Paul always ordered coffee, no food. Years later, I asked Paul about that. He told me that he wanted to treat me well, though he had little spending money. In those days, there was curbside service, so we never left the car. Sonic Drive-Ins have resurrected the concept. One night when we returned to my sorority house, Paul parked on the side street next to a row of hedges. We sat there talking about our future. Then Paul began crying, "Barbara, we'll never be able to afford to be together."

I had heard him express concerns and worries; this was the first time I had seen him cry.

"Paul, that's not true. We both will be working after we graduate. Why are you talking about this now?"

"Nothing has ever worked out for me."

"Please don't cry. We'll find a way. I know it."

"I don't think so".

"I can't take this negativity anymore. You're making me stressed. I don't want to be with you when you are like this."

I left him sitting in the car as I slammed the door and stormed into the house.

As in previous times, when I became angry with him, Paul would perk up, return to his fun loving self, and promise to be less negative. His relentless pursuit began again. As usual, I gave in. We continued seeing each other exclusively. At this point Paul decided to call me Snuffy as an endearment. I have no idea why he liked this name. The only Snuffy I knew about was the cartoon character Snuffy Smith, whom I definitely did not then, and do not now, resemble. I still have a face powder compact and a souvenir beer mug on which he had engraved the name Snuffy. Thinking back, I never again heard that term of endearment after we were married and don't know why.

I always knew where to locate Paul between classes. He would be at the SUP Store holding court. I could always find him surrounded by a circle of friends listening to his jokes, laughing, and interacting with him. Sometimes Paul skipped classes to entertain his many admirers, even though he knew I strongly disapproved. Everyone seemed to like and respect my future husband. The fraternity elected him to various leadership positions, and eventually, president.

It did not take much enticement for his frat brothers to cast Paul as the lead character in a spoof of the classic tale, "Anastasia", renamed "Amnesia" for the annual fraternity entertainment challenge, Jason's Jamboree. Paul was perfect for the role. The event took place at Foster Auditorium, the location of our first date. Students and faculty packed the place, enjoying all of the fraternities' presentations. Then the brothers of AEPi came on stage. Paul, dressed in drag, cavorted in the title role for at least a quarter hour before finally resting on his toilet throne, while the throng laughed and applauded. I sat as far back in the auditorium as possible. At the time, I was embarrassed. What a prude Snuffy was then. They were a hit!

The following February Paul gave me a fraternity pin at an AEPi formal dance. The photo we had taken that night is special to me. His loving arms around me made me feel protected and happy. "Barbara," he said, "this isn't my pin. I lost mine and had to order a new one. I asked my friend, Harry, if I could use his until my new pin arrives. I didn't want to wait." It was okay with me. However, I have a suspicion I was technically pinned to Harry for a while.

February became our special month. Paul sent Valentine cards almost each day for a week before the actual holiday. Until a year before his death, I received a bouquet of flowers every Valentine's Day. When our daughters were older, he also brought bouquets to them.

Everyone understood pinning was the symbol of a commitment to be engaged for marriage. Once Paul determined that he and I did have a future together, he wasted no additional summer breaks languishing in New York. Paul found a part-time job selling women's shoes in Stein's Shoe Store in downtown Tuscaloosa and attended summer school classes in order to graduate as quickly as possible.

Paul studied hard and continued working. I have the letters he wrote to me during one summer and a few from one year's winter break. I looked forward to receiving them and seeing his silly ways of addressing the envelopes, such as Miss Adorable

Vogel or Miss Snuffy Vogel. The postman must have thought that at least one of us was strange. When I was unhappy or depressed he wrote of his love and encouragement. What a turnabout! This made me feel more secure in my decision to stay with him.

In July of 1958, he wrote:

". . . My only ambition in life is to spend it with you, loving and caring for you. As long as blood flows in my veins and breath enters my lungs I will only live to do for you. You know the part of the marriage ceremony that goes for better or worse. There is no worse, for to be with you makes me better, us better, and even the world looks better. Better or worse as far as I am concerned is only different degrees of best when I know that I have you. Dear, although the present is filled with material doubt, I know we will reach our goal, because, we have the intangible, love. Or is it intangible? You know, I can feel it. I have it inside me and my fingertips tingle with love's vibration. I see it in every day. I wake up and it is beside me. It is part of all I do. Love is only intangible to those who do not have it. Think how lucky we are. To know that soon we will be together. To know that in the near future we will live together as man and wife. These things make my life worth living."

'Twas a woman who drove me to drink.
I never even had the courtesy to thank her.

W.C. Fields
Comedian/writer

No woman caused Paul's drinking, as far as I know. Yet, the source of the quote is appropriate. Paul loved to imitate W.C. Fields. I can see him now, pretending to flip an imaginary cigar, and hear him addressing some unknown female companion, "my little chickadee." There was uninhibited drinking on campus. All fraternity events involved alcohol, specifically the purple passion concoction prepared for Alpha Epsilon Pi's annual Hawaiian Weekend. Many students got drunk at parties that were almost weekly events.

Both of my parents were social drinkers. I drank alcohol along with everyone else, but could take it or leave it. Paul's capacity to imbibe large amounts of liquor should have worried me, but I naively accepted this as normal behavior because everyone I knew drank. One Saturday when Paul and I had plans for later in the day, I received a telephone call from an AEPi fraternity brother, "Paul won't be there for a while. He had too much to drink. He's sleeping it off. He'll call you later." I was extremely upset. The pattern of Paul's misbehavior followed by extreme remorse started back then. I did not recognize it as a major problem; I wish I had.

Later in 1959 when he was completing school after I had graduated and was back in Mobile, Paul wrote the following to me:

"Last night when I came home from work I was greeted by my roommate and a half case of beer. Of course, I had some beer, but I became melancholy and sentimental. I went over to get a friend and both of us went and had a beer in every joint in town. We told each other our troubles and got quite loaded. It was a good evening for me because I got loose and didn't worry so much as usual with me."

He considered this a good evening. There were many more 'good' evenings to come. Paul told me not too many years before his death, that he believed he would die if he did not drink. Now I understand what he meant. Paul truly believed drinking helped him function; he was self-medicating.

The family is one of nature's masterpieces.

George Santayana
Philosopher/essayist

MOBILE, ALABAMA

I cannot recall ever receiving a formal marriage proposal. Paul and I just had the understanding that we would eventually marry. I was impressed, and so were my parents, that Paul insisted on speaking to my father. I remember that evening well. We were at my home in Mobile during one of our school breaks in 1959. Often we would watch television with my parents after dinner. This time Paul and I had another plan. He was very nervous as he asked my dad, "Mr. Vogel, may I speak with you privately?" Paul took a drink and then he and my dad stepped into our den, a small room next to the kitchen. I stayed away at a discreet distance, straining to hear the conversation.

My mom was busy cleaning up the kitchen. With her back to everyone, my mother had no idea what was going on while she was washing the dishes. I was helping her by drying dishes while trying not to look in Paul's direction. He wanted to get my dad's blessing, although we both knew that it was a bit old-fashioned to do that. I respected the fact that this was important to Paul. I had no doubt that my father would approve, which he did. Both of my parents liked Paul and were pleased to know that we would marry. "Barbara, you know I can't afford to buy a ring," Paul commented. I assured him, "I know that. I don't need a ring to be engaged."

Though somewhat disappointed, I had hope for our future. I intended to keep positive thoughts. I had not met Paul's parents, though we had talked on the telephone a number of times. After my college graduation the following May, my parents, Paul, and I drove to New York City. The trip was a graduation gift for me, as well as an opportunity to meet Paul's family.

New York, New York

Dad was a cautious driver. However, once we got onto the multilane freeway into New York City, my dad asked, "Paul, will you drive?" I didn't expect that he would make such a request. Dad usually wanted to be in charge; this time he was unaccustomed to driving with numerous automobiles whizzing by. I wondered about that decision. Paul had never driven in New York. His family used public transportation, as did most New Yorkers. Traffic there was quite different from Clovis, Mobile, or Tuscaloosa. I guess Dad thought Paul would be less intimidated by the traffic. I suspected that my dad and mom were silently praying. I just held my breath and hoped for the best. All went well and we got into the city without incident.

My family and I stayed at a hotel in Manhattan. The room was extremely small, barely enough space for three people. This was my first trip to New York. Paul, of course, stayed with his folks.

One morning Paul met us at the hotel for breakfast in the snack shop. He wore a blue knit shirt with nice slacks, looking very handsome. The hostess approached us. "Sir, I'm sorry, you have to wear a jacket." I thought, you have to be kidding. She provided an ill-fitting jacket for Paul and we proceeded to our table. The request was so pretentious, why require a jacket in a coffee shop? My first impression of New York City wasn't very positive.

Several days later, Paul arranged for me to meet him and his mom in the afternoon at a downtown jewelry store. She told me that she and Paul's dad wanted me to choose a cocktail ring for my graduation gift. I took a taxi to the designated location, wearing a tomato-red cotton dress that looked good on me. Paul beamed when I emerged from the vehicle. He was grinning from ear-to-ear. To be truthful, I was excited, very nervous, and a bit ill at ease. Paul held my hand as we entered the small shop.

The jeweler brought out several trays of rings. I didn't know what to choose; all of the rings were lovely. I certainly did not want to be extravagant, but had no guidelines. Paul's mom said, "Barbara, pick out the ring you like." Paul wasn't giving me much help. Since I would not immediately make a selection from the several trays of rings presented to me, she said to the jeweler, "Don't you have another tray to show her?" To my astonishment, he brought out a large tray that contained diamond engagement rings. I looked at Paul; Paul looked at me and shrugged his shoulders as if to say he didn't know what his mother was doing.

Lillian Paper had her plan and was a determined lady. She insisted I choose from this tray. By that time, I was shaking. I found a perfect ring, just what I always wanted—an emerald cut diamond with two diamond baguettes on each side in a platinum setting. Paul was stunned. I was in shock. At the time, the ring fit my finger perfectly. It had to be resized later. I suppose my hand wanted that particular ring to fit right then and there. After Lillian paid the sales clerk, I walked out of the store with a beautiful ring on my left hand. I was engaged—to Paul or his mother?

Typical of my prudent future mother-in-law, she dragged us to another friendly jeweler for an appraisal, just to be certain she had gotten a good deal. That evening my parents and Paul's family finally met at their apartment in Manhattan to celebrate our engagement. The apartment was small. I remember climbing stairs to the upper floor apartment entrance. The outside of the building looked cold and intimidating. Yet, from the moment we entered their home, the warmth and joy of Paul's family enveloped us. Paul's sister, Jackie, her husband, Irving, and Paul's aunt and uncle were also there. We enjoyed a beautiful decorated cake from the family bakery to commemorate the occasion.

Paul was unable to complete his studies in time for spring graduation. Therefore, it was necessary for him to continue until January. I began teaching school in Mobile in September. Paul came to see me as often as he could, usually on a bus. Sometimes he was able to find an automobile ride. Other times he drove his old jalopy with the hope it would not break down.

During this time, I was living with my parents until our wedding day. I remember Paul told me, "I counted the breaks in the pavement on Dauphin Street to remember when to turn onto your street." Being apart wasn't easy for either of us. Even though we were busy, we missed being together.

We're all here for a spell, get all the good laughs you can.

Will Rogers
Comedian/humorist

MOBILE, ALABAMA

One ordinary evening during one of his visits, Paul and I drove from my parents' home to pick up fried chicken baskets for the four of us. I sat in the front passenger seat carefully guarding the dinners. We made our way through a quiet residential neighborhood. Out of nowhere, a car plowed into the driver's side of my parents' Ford sedan. Chicken, biscuits, French fried potatoes, and coleslaw went flying everywhere.

"Paul, what happened?"

"That car ran through the stop sign. Are you okay?"

"I hit my knees on the dashboard. Nothing is broken."

I limped over to a home on the corner to use a phone to report the accident to the police and let my folks know what had happened. This was before the time of mandatory seat belts and cell phones. Paul was unhurt and remained at the accident site to be certain no one was injured in the child-filled car that hit us. The woman driving told him no one was hurt.

Upon my return to the scene, I could hardly restrain a chuckle, though I was a bit shaken by the event and later needed some medical attention for my bruised knee. There was Paul, one bent elbow casually resting on the corner lamppost, munching on a chicken leg held in his other hand. Nothing could deter him when he was hungry.

Paul graduated in January 1960 and began working for an accounting firm in Mobile. He lived in a rented room next door to our home. The marriage license clerk at Mobile City Hall remarked, "How nice to be marrying the boy-next-door." We didn't have the heart to correct him. Our wedding took place in Mobile the following June at the Spring Hill Avenue Temple, a Reform Jewish congregation.

We planned our honeymoon on a shoestring budget and were pleased that the New York relatives traditionally gave money as wedding gifts; those gifts made our trip possible. During these years, Southerners typically gave wrapped gifts, such as serving pieces, china, crystal, and kitchenware—the needs of newlyweds. Many brides enjoyed displaying the assortment of presents before the wedding. Therefore, my parents' living/dining room glittered like a gift shop. Paul asked, "What are we going to do with so many silver serving pieces?" I knew; polish them.

Panama City, Florida was our intended honeymoon destination. After spending the first evening in Pensacola, Paul and I made our way to Panama City, ending up at the Barney Gray Motel. The best I can say is that it was a beachfront motel. The building was old and not in the best of condition, but it was what we could afford. The squeaky bedsprings caused me some embarrassment. On our first night there, Paul wanted to go to a nearby nightclub. It had a large windmill on the front. We had a few drinks and an unexpected floorshow. A stripper gyrated around the floor and looked like she had an eye for Paul. I was not amused and got Paul out of there as soon as possible. We did enjoy our week's stay at the beach resort. Paul was happy and, thank goodness, sober for the entire vacation.

All marriages are happy. It's the living together afterward that causes all the trouble.

> Raymond Hull
> Canadian playwright

When we returned to Mobile, our wedded life began, as did many couples, in a nice, rather small apartment. I continued teaching. Several of our married friends also lived in the apartment complex. Paul seemed contented with his new job as an apprentice accountant. I decided to teach at our congregation's religious school on Sunday mornings, in addition to my regular public school teaching position during the week. Paul spent those mornings cooking delicious lunches for us to enjoy upon my return. I did the cleanup chores without objection. Entertaining friends, bowling with our congregational league, and enjoying family events occupied much of our leisure time. We often found things to laugh about, something we always had in common. We could find pleasure in ordinary activities and humor in the silliest circumstances.

Aunt Marion and Uncle Herman Vogel brought a special ashtray from overseas. Originally, they had it in their home. Printed on it were the words, luxardo mara chino. Paul loved to say those words over and over and over again with the best Italian accent he could muster. I had no idea what the words meant, nor did Paul. He just loved the lilting sound as he spoke the words. Knowing the fun Paul had with the accented phrase, they gave it to Paul for his office.

I must confess that I, too, often repeat the words now when I spy the piece on a table in my current living area. It is fun to say, "luxardo mara chino." However, my Italian accent isn't as charming as was Paul's. I recently learned that the ashtray probably advertised Luxardo Maraschino Liqueur.

One evening we were entertaining some close friends at our apartment. One of the guys was in the military and was reassigned to Kwajalein Island in the Pacific where there was a U.S. Navy Base left from WWII. "I know your job will be to stand on the beach and catch the rockets directed at the island," joked one of the guests. All of us broke out in uproarious laughter. Perhaps time dulls the humor, but not the happy memory of that evening relaxing with friends.

One time the source of our amusement began as a bad situation. We went through a period of time when the plumbing in our apartment took a turn for the worse—an understatement. The upstairs neighbor's toilet began emptying into our bathtub. I will not detail the results of that catastrophe. It took several days to correct the problem. I can't recall just how many times I scrubbed the bathtub before I would set my foot in it. I never felt comfortable tub bathing as before; that was the beginning of my preference for showers.

Another time in the middle of the night, a loud knocking on our front door woke us up. We couldn't imagine what that was about. At first I was wary. Paul went to the door. "Be careful," I warned. To his astonishment, there stood our across the hall neighbor in her rather flimsy nightgown. "Please help me," she pleaded. "My husband has been drinking and I'm afraid." It seemed he had hit her. She asked Paul to go into her apartment with her. He turned to me.

"Honey, do you think I should go?"

"I don't know. The guy could be angry with you for butting in."

"I know. I'll go, but come back if things get out of hand."

"Paul, please be careful."

When Paul returned, he told me that the husband was in a drunken stupor on their bed. You can imagine what was going through our minds that night. As a young newlywed, I wasn't very happy to see a scantily clad woman on my doorstep. In retrospect, it was rather amusing to watch how my husband handled the situation. He was uncomfortable, but put forth his best take-charge attitude.

*I was always complaining about
the ruts in the road, until I realized
that the ruts are the road.*

Author unknown

Paul's happiness came to a sudden halt with the serious illness of his father. It was a cold night in December 1960. We were in line to buy tickets at a downtown movie theater in Mobile. Suddenly, from out of nowhere Uncle Herman came up to us.

"Paul, your mother called. Your father has had a heart attack." "We must leave now," said Paul. I agreed and we immediately went home so Paul could arrange to fly to New York. I remember how upset he was at the news; he and his father were very close.

Paul returned when it seemed his father was doing better, but not long after, the ultimate bad news arrived. He took another quick trip to New York to attend his dad's funeral. Harry Paper was only 53 years old when he died. This experience was excruciating for my husband. I believe this was the first time Paul had experienced the death of someone so close to him.

He did not handle it very well. We argued when Paul refused to acknowledge memorial donations for his father.

"Paul, it's appropriate to send thank you notes."
"No, I won't."
"I don't understand."
"I don't care."
"I'll write them for you."
"No! I don't want to talk about it any further."

We wrote no thank you notes. I regret that I didn't go ahead and do it in spite of what Paul said.

Disappointments are to the soul what the thunderstorm is to the air.

> Friedrich von Schiller
> Philosopher/writer

The second time Paul went to New York for the funeral, I stayed with my parents. I really did not feel like spending more evenings alone in our apartment. When he returned, Paul held me tightly as if I were going to leave him, too. We were in my parents' guest room. It seemed strange to be a guest in my former home.

Paul had promised his mother that he would attend Sabbath worship every week for the following year to recite Kaddish for his father. (Kaddish is a Jewish prayer that praises God in remembrance of the deceased.) Paul was not a usual weekly worshiper. Nonetheless, he never missed a Sabbath service for that entire year; he kept his promise, even when the only attendees on Saturday morning were little old ladies and Paul. His devotion impressed me.

Paul and I did not want to stay in the apartment forever. We were able to buy a small home in north Mobile using a veteran's loan. It was new and suited our needs. By the beginning of 1963

I was pregnant with our first child. I continued teaching through the year and enjoyed my pregnancy.

In June we traveled with my parents to my mother's family reunion in Little Rock, Arkansas. Although I was five months pregnant, I handled the car trip fairly well and was grateful that Paul agreed to come. It was the first time he attended an out-of-town family event. I was embarrassed to acknowledge that Paul was too busy to join us at most happy family occasions during the years following.

Our first child arrived in October 1963. It was an exciting, happy time. Paul reveled in his new role. I was a full-time mother. When I took our baby, Hara Dee, who was named to honor her late grandfather Harry, for her first month checkup, my father accompanied me. Paul told me he had to work. I remember the day, Friday, November 22, 1963, because of President John F. Kennedy's assassination in Dallas, TX. The television in the doctor's waiting room focused on reporting the sad events.

Our second daughter arrived in 1966. I received a dozen pink roses from Paul with each birth. He insisted each time that he give his baby girls their first baths. I'm glad to report that our second daughter's first month check-up did not coincide with any traumatic national event. However, to the regret of their fans, August 1966 was the last live concert given by The Beatles.

All was going very well. In 1964, Paul became a full partner in the accounting firm—a professional milestone. My husband accepted the presidency of the men's club of our congregation, did an outstanding job, and tried to be a responsible participant in congregational life. One time he was a bit embarrassed when introducing a visiting speaker, a member of the clergy. He introduced the guest by listing his many accomplishments including having attended the Reform Jewish Cemetery. Of course, he meant seminary. Oh well, he told me it was a good laugh for all.

Paul was supportive of my taking a part-time job to become the director of our congregation's religious school. I had quit full-time school teaching when our first child arrived. He took care of the girls on Sunday mornings and had lunch prepared when I arrived home.

At this point in life Paul enjoyed being a family man, even taking up golf for stress relief. Paul bought a left-handed set of clubs and played the course when he could. I cannot say he was very good at it, though he tried. Once I accompanied him as he played the nine holes. It was a limited course and a very long walk. I would say Paul's path from each tee to green was a zigzag of lengthy proportions, not at all like the golfers who managed to hit the balls in a straight line. From then on, I encouraged him from afar.

During this time Paul worked at taking better care of himself by losing weight, though he would not give up his excessive smoking habit. We entertained friends often as possible. I think this was the peak of Paul's adult life. He looked great and played the role of family man as well as he could. I deliberately use the term play. In retrospect, I wonder if he was really cut out to be the head of a family or if his increasing mental instability just made his desire too difficult a challenge.

I don't know if there was a point in time when our social lives began to disintegrate. Slowly he found reasons to be only with business associates. Paul would accompany me to some events in my social world, but did not call anyone in this circle his friend. His problem drinking began again a few years later. Having only one full income and two extra mouths to feed strained our finances. Paul was making progress in his career, but found it caused him major stress. There were many nights when he did not come home until the wee hours of the morning after a night of drinking with friends. I spent numerous sleepless nights telephoning hospital emergency rooms to see if he had been in an accident.

One evening he gave me a heads up. "Don't expect me to be home for dinner. In fact, I don't know how late I will be." Paul was a skilled billiards player. On this night, he and his best friend played an entire evening at an acquaintance's home. It was a challenge match with high stakes betting going on. Of course, I had no idea where he was or what he was doing until the next day.

The next morning I received a telephone call from Paul. He said, "Meet me at the mall around noon. We'll have lunch together." When I arrived, I saw Paul and his billiards buddy with his wife seated at the restaurant, waiting for me to arrive. I joined them. Paul presented me with a beautiful gold and gem-studded cocktail ring, bought with the money he had won. I wasn't pleased with the source of the funds, but never could say no to a gift from Paul. It was typical of Paul to buy something for me as his expression of penance and love. I didn't know whether to be angry or grateful. Paul's luck did not last forever.

After a night of drinking with friends, his head went through the windshield when he ran his car into a parking lot lamppost during a heavy rain, ending up in the hospital. My cousin, who was with Paul at the time, called. "Paul was in an accident; I think he will be okay." It was a frightening time for me, but Paul quickly recovered from a minor head wound. I was relieved that no one filed any charges; it was just an accident.

With our bills mounting, we decided it would be best that I return to classroom teaching. I really did not want to go back to work, but knew I needed to do it. I enjoyed being a stay-at-home mom. One evening Paul and I were in bed discussing the logistics of getting the girls to and from school. Then we heard Hara crying in her bedroom. Paul and I went to her. I sat on the bed and put my arms around her. Paul was standing close by.

"Honey, what's wrong?"

"Are you going to give me away?"

"What? We aren't going to give you away. We'd never give you away; we love you. You're our daughter. What made you think that?"

"I heard you ask Daddy who was going to take me."

"Hara, I asked your father about who was going to take you to school.

"Oh," Hara replied. That encounter did not help me feel any better about returning to work. It upset me. We were fortunate to find a reliable and loving housekeeper to help at home and care for the girls while we were away.

The worst evening for me was when Paul unexpectedly stayed out all night. In the morning, it was almost time for me to leave for school, and no one was there to watch the children until my housekeeper arrived. I paced the floor, checking the clock every few minutes, and then checking the driveway to see if he was home. I finally heard the car door slam shut. With a voice louder than normal I asked, "Paul, where have you been? I've been so worried; I thought something happened to you. Why didn't you call? I have to go to work." I left in anger, having received no answers from Paul.

God hath given you one face,
and you make yourselves another.

William Shakespeare
Playwright

Heavy drinking followed by irritability and then deep sleep was an increasing pattern of Paul's behavior. I was unsure of what to do. He rebuffed my repeated attempts to discuss my concerns. He never would openly discuss his actions or activities with me. Again, I foolishly put aside my fear when his behavior would return to some normalcy. I had put myself in the role of enabler without understanding its ramifications. In other words, I had become codependent. I made excuses or looked the other way to present a public image of a whole, healthy, and functioning family. Inwardly I was as embarrassed as I was fearful.

Having been raised in a dysfunctional family led to my not being able to solve many of the challenges I faced during my years with Paul. There are categories of people vulnerable to low self-esteem. I think that defines who I was—raised in an environment where feelings were not openly expressed or welcomed in an inflexible environment. It wasn't difficult to begin a relationship and marry someone who was dependent on alcohol, food, and was a workaholic. It was difficult living with a disturbed individual.

Paul and I bought land in a newly developed subdivision in a very nice part of town. One afternoon we were surveying our property and discussing the future home we wanted to build. The children were with us. Hara was annoying her sister, as siblings often do, trying to kick her. Paul's reaction was swift as he suddenly and harshly grabbed her arm and severely reprimanded her. It was the first time I saw him behave so intensely with his daughter. "Paul, stop!" I yelled, as I grabbed his arm to restrain him. I saw frightened looks on the girls' faces. This had been a happy afternoon turned sour. We left in silence.

Money often costs too much.

Ralph Waldo Emerson
Author

Several years later, around 1973, we began working on the plans to build our new home. It was a stressful time, but Paul and I had fun sharing in the planning and overseeing the construction. In my mind, this was a new beginning for us. I cherished the times together sitting at the dining table, poring over the floor plan of our future home, making joint decisions of how it would look. We were bonding as never before. There were no arguments about our choices of interior design and decoration. To me the completed house was lovely and I thought our lives might take an upward turn towards happiness and stability.

We prepared for and enjoyed several family milestones in our new home. Paul enjoyed entertaining. He avidly read anything in print, particularly cookbooks. One year he subscribed to a gourmet magazine; he also joined the Cheese of the Month Club. We had an unusual assortment of cheese knives that came with the monthly cheese selection. I never did figure out what to do with so many little knives.

Paul appreciated a truly well prepared meal and delighted in browsing through cooking utensil departments or specialty stores. Even as cooking was a pleasure for him, cleaning up was another story—not.

Occasionally Paul found time to share his gastronomic talents with his family and friends. One of his most memorable meals was a fruit stuffed goose with potatoes on the side. My advice is never allow anyone to cook a goose inside your kitchen. I believe every surface of our oven and kitchen counter tops had a slippery layer of goose fat. It was a daunting clean-up job for me. Maybe that is where the expression, *your goose is cooked*, originated.

In his attempt to find an avenue for bringing in more income, Paul involved himself in a venture that brought him together with other investors and businessmen. There were numerous meetings followed by evenings of drinking, of course. Instead of supplying start-up funds, Paul offered his accounting advice and services to the new upscale men's clothing store in Mobile's primary mall. As before, I faced Paul's erratic hours. His mood swings became more frequent and occasional bouts of heavy drinking continued. A significant concern of mine was that we no longer had any mutual friends. His good friends were business associates with whom I had nothing in common. I attended various social events with Paul, but never felt comfortable being there.

We took few vacations as a family. Paul was obsessed with his accounting practice and need to earn money. One of our infrequent vacations was to Disney World, because it coincided with a professional meeting in Orlando. The girls and I had a great time, as did Paul. I know we should have had more of these family times together, but didn't.

Working long hours is just one symptom of depression. Obsessive behavior is common with persons exhibiting mental health issues. It can be excessive smoking and/or eating or spending beyond their means. Some people become compulsive gamblers. That is the only activity that never became a problem for Paul, even though he did love winning at the all night billiards challenge.

Why don't more men seek help? Many believe that it is a sign of weakness to admit they need help. Men should tough it out in silence. If a man cries, he is not manly. The stigma for males inhibits their seeking help. My late husband was the perfect example; he could not/would not get treatment, no matter how I urgently pleaded that he do so. In retrospect, it would have been wise if I had made an appointment for him.

Depression is a prison where you are both the suffering prisoner and the cruel jailer.

Dr. Dorothy Rowe
Psychologist/author

One weekend in 1975, my parents agreed to take care of the girls while Paul and I went to a resort to celebrate our wedding anniversary. I looked forward to a romantic getaway in Pensacola, Florida, about an hour's drive from Mobile. The motel was on beachfront property. We enjoyed dinner and dancing, but as usual, Paul was drinking too much.

All of a sudden, he arbitrarily said, "We are leaving." I begged him, "Paul, please don't end the evening. It's our anniversary. It's still early." He refused to compromise and began walking back to our room as I continued to follow behind—pleading with him—while trying to keep up with his rapid pace. Upon entering the room, Paul collapsed on the bed and immediately fell sound asleep in a drunken stupor, not waking until the next morning. Disappointment consumed me and I cried from that evening until we arrived home the next day. On the way back, Paul tried to apologize.

"We're going to stop for a nice brunch; I know I screwed up. I'm sorry. Please stop crying."

"I can't; I was looking forward to this weekend together."

"I don't know what else to say. I really am sorry."

"Paul, this keeps happening."

During this period that side of Paul's disturbed personality reappeared, being unreasonably provoked resulting in aggressive behavior. There had been previous brief bursts of his temper, just as he had the afternoon while looking over our property with our daughters. Again, he directed his anger towards Hara, who was beginning to exhibit her own disturbed behavior. I often wonder if Paul was seeing himself in her actions.

There were two other occasions when Paul became physically aggressive towards Hara. Being a rebellious teenager, she and her dad were arguing about something she had or had not done or said; the details are unimportant. They were in our hallway when I heard a loud commotion. The two of them were face-to-face, screaming at each other. To me it seemed that Paul was ready to attack her. I stepped between them and yelled something at both of them. Paul backed down. Hara quickly retreated to her bedroom, slamming the door behind her. I stood there shaking. I don't know if Paul would have hurt her. He had never been a violent man, but it was obvious he now had little self-control.

On another evening Paul, our girls, and I were enjoying dinner at home. Hara made some remark that Paul found unacceptable. All I recall is that he reached across the table in a threatening way and put his hands to her throat. I yelled, "Paul, you're choking her." His reply was, "I'm not choking her, but trying to stop her words."

I know he loved his children, but he could not suppress his bursts of anger. I should have sought help right then and there. Unlike today when one can search the Internet and find multiple resources and information, during the 70s there were few places to seek help on one's own. If he wasn't throwing ashtrays, then my husband was verbally abusive to Hara and me. For some reason he left our younger daughter alone. Paul was gradually becoming out of touch with our feelings and concerns.

Glass, China and Reputation are easily cracked and never well mended.

> Benjamin Franklin

I was so afraid to allow Paul's problem to become public. It could jeopardize his career. I spoke with a close friend who sympathized, but could offer no practical solution. What was I to do? I was torn between my responsibilities to my children and my love for the man I married. Should I divorce him? I was afraid that I couldn't make it on my own. The girls pleaded with me to leave him. I could not; I didn't want to cause Paul any additional pain. I loved him and remembered how he used to be. Once I confidentially spoke with an attorney to learn about my options. I thought that legal separation, rather than divorce, might be a possibility. The lawyer told me legal separation wasn't available in Alabama.

I did not realize what I was doing at the time. I truly fit the profile of a person in the enabling behavior role. I found the following list of statements at www.coping.us to define an enabler. I said all of these to myself or my girls at one time or another:

I'm going to give him another chance.

I love him; I can't leave him.

I don't want him to suffer any pain or hurt.
I made my vows for life; I could never leave him.
He doesn't care how much he hurts us by his behavior.
I feel so unappreciated.

Rabbi Perkins, whom I mentioned previously, explained, "Once upon a time, Jews found it hard to believe that there were any Jewish alcoholics. Denial was a natural, conventional response to the suggestion that Jews might also be susceptible to alcoholism or other addictions. Now, we know better, and yet still many Jews feel ashamed to admit that they or members of their family suffer from chemical dependency." This, of course, is not limited to those of the Jewish faith. Families of any group experience the same struggles.

Paul challenged me. "Barbara, I will go to jail rather than give you any money if you leave me." He may have been bluffing, but I did not want to test him. I became afraid as his behavior towards me became more intimidating.

One evening I tried to leave in my car to go to an important appointment following a fundraising event. I dressed and proceeded to the carport. Paul followed me, attempting to block the door.

"You aren't leaving."

"But Paul, I have to be there. I have responsibilities.

"No, you're not going."

"Don't be ridiculous. I have to pick up the money to be banked."

I finally managed to leave the house and move towards my car as Paul followed, trying to block the car door, and restraining my arm while demanding, "Get away from the car!"

"Paul, please move. I have to go!"

"I don't want you to go."

"What I have to do won't take long."

"Don't go!"

"What's wrong with you? You are being unreasonable. I'm leaving now; don't try to stop me!"

After what seemed an eternity—but was probably no more than a half hour—shaken by the confrontation, I finally was able to break free from his grip, get in the car, and leave. Paul said no more about it to me when I returned. I was furious. His silence was overwhelming. What was going to happen next? Could this be the same person who wrote such loving letters and unfailingly pursued me all over the University of Alabama campus?

I felt some ray of hope when I scheduled counseling sessions for Hara. She was exhibiting self-destructive behavior. Biting herself to the point of drawing blood was another symptom of her illness. She also cut herself with razors. Mental health professionals explain that this is self-injurious behavior (SIB). I once asked her, "Why do you do this to yourself?" Her reply was, "When I feel pain, I feel alive." At one point, her psychiatric counselor wanted Paul to attend sessions with her. Good, I thought to myself, perhaps he can help both of them. However, as soon as the discussions came too close to discussing his problems, Paul told me, "I have no more time to attend." He quit going.

I tried talking with two of Paul's clients who were good friends and trusted professional men, hoping they could convince Paul to seek medical help. Paul was a very good actor. He convinced both of them that I was overreacting. The people from whom we most need support often wear blinders. I was on an emotional roller coaster that never stopped. I believed I couldn't get off.

Then forces of nature intervened in the form of Hurricane Frederick. I will never forget that 1979 storm; it was brutal. Paul had no firsthand experience getting ready for a hurricane. Once, ten years earlier, Hurricane Camille threatened our area; we went to the home of my aunt and uncle. Camille did not directly hit Mobile. Paul told me, "I remember a severe storm in New York when I was a child. However, the only downed trees were in Central Park." The forecast was that Hurricane Frederick would hit Mobile directly. I was trying to prepare the house. Paul was not there. He had done the same thing years before when we had a freak snowstorm in Mobile.

⁂

On that cold winter morning around 1967, I stepped out to the driveway to retrieve our morning newspaper. It was about 7:00 a.m. I nearly broke my neck slipping on black ice, a thin, unexpected, invisible coating of ice on a road or walkway surface. Then it began snowing. It snowed all day, which I had never seen happen in Mobile. I was trying to deal with the children at home, expecting Paul to arrive home from the office at any time. He returned late in the day when the roads were not safe for travel.

"Paul, what have you been doing all day? I've been worried."

"A bunch of guys in the building were playing cards. I joined the game."

"You should have come home."

It was as if he were in denial that there was any danger. Mental illness can cause its victims to increase risky behavior.

⁂

Now it was September 10, 1979. Paul wasn't home and I was doing all I could to prepare our house for the impending storm. My mother was there with me. My father was attending an out-of-town conference.

Finally, Paul came home before Frederick hit. Paul, our girls, my mother, and I spent most of the evening sitting in the dark confines of our hallway, the only place where there were no windows. The power had failed early in the evening. Paul and I grabbed two flashlights and took turns checking the interior ceilings for leaks. He put buckets to catch the dripping water in several damaged places in our dining room ceiling. Through the night, we sat with our backs against the vibrating hallway walls while the winds howled and the hurricane did its damage outside. It was a long, scary, and exhausting night. In the early morning hours, when the winds seemed to calm down, we finally dragged ourselves to bed.

Around four o'clock in the morning a persistent knocking on our front door woke us from our sleep. Who in the world could that be? I opened it to discover my father standing there, grateful to be safely home. He said he had rented a car in Chicago because no airlines were flying into our city. "I've been driving around for hours trying to find your house. All street lights were out," he told us. Even though he had lived in Mobile for forty years, the familiar landscape had been rearranged, as if he were in a strange city. "I was really scared," he said.

When daylight came, we found we had no extensive damage. Many of our neighbors were not so fortunate. Part of our next door neighbor's roof had crashed into the front windows of the house across the street. The entire town was in disarray with downed trees and severely damaged homes. Everyone had to cope with the loss of power for several weeks. Fortunately, it was

September and still warm weather. I had an all-electric kitchen and had always thought our outdoor gas grill would be an emergency backup. I was wrong. It was another victim of Frederick, out of commission. However, Paul was a good sport and helped by cooking on the patio using a borrowed hibachi grill. I stood in long lines at a local supermarket to pick up bags of ice to get us through the hot days. Through it all, Paul surprised me when he seemed to take these problems in stride. He was thankful that we all were safe.

The *Azalea City News and Review* had a special September 15 issue with hurricane photos and features. It said this was Mobile's number one weather event of the seventies. According to Dr. Bill Williams, a broadcast weatherman specializing in climatology, Frederick was an unusual storm. It had a remarkably large eye that expanded to about forty miles as it approached the coast. He reported that he had never heard of one that big. The headline of *The Mobile Press Register* on Tuesday, September 18, 1979, was "Fear, Numbness Bow to Hope for Future." That is how we all felt.

Because of the considerable tree damage throughout our community, there were numerous trucks carrying logs coming and going all over town. One midweek day, a huge truck loaded with long logs confronted Paul as he was driving from work during his lunch break. The truck unexpectedly pulled out in front of his car on a main thoroughfare, blocking all lanes of escape. Paul's small Pontiac Sunbird plowed into the truck, throwing Paul through the windshield. He luckily escaped serious injury again; he could have easily been decapitated. A night in the hospital with some minor head wounds got Paul back on his feet. The accident totaled his new car. I was surprised to find this episode did not put Paul in his usual downward spiral of depression.

He took the insurance money and bought a Pontiac Grand Prix, the largest model made by General Motors. According to Paul, it would be a bit safer inside a larger vehicle. Otherwise, he quipped, "If this doesn't protect me, I will have to purchase a Sherman tank!"

After that, life for the Paper family was at last moving along rather uneventfully. Paul was busy with his work and beginning the cycle of tax season with extended office hours. The storm had frightened Paul in a way I had not before seen. "Barb, I will try to be more responsible. I promise to stop drinking so much. I will try to quit smoking." I was satisfied that he was serious this time. However, in February 1980, fate brought us face-to-face with our ultimate challenge.

*And now my soul is poured out within me;
Days of affliction have taken hold upon me.*

> Book of Job 30:16

It was Mardi Gras Day 1980, also known as Fat Tuesday. Mobile, named the Mother of Mystics, was the first to celebrate Mardi Gras in the United States. A good friend and I were at the downtown parades. The day was nice and clear, not too cold for February. I arrived home in the late afternoon. As soon as I walked in the door, I heard the telephone ringing.

"Hello."
"With whom am I speaking?"
"This is Barbara Paper."
"Are you Mrs. Paul Paper?"
"Yes, I am."
A voice on the other end told me, "I am an emergency room nurse at Springhill Memorial Hospital. Your husband is here. He was in a car accident, but is not in immediate danger."
"I'm on my way."
With my heart in my throat, I found Paul lying on a gurney with a bewildered look on his face. To me the scene was like a

replay of previous hospital visits. "I don't know what happened," he told me. "I remember the emergency team helping me. I was thrown out of the car. Then I blacked out. I don't remember arriving at the hospital. Barbara, get the police report tomorrow. I don't know if this was my fault or not."

I had always dreaded the possibility that Paul's drunken driving would cause a deadly accident. Chronic alcoholism is progressive. A friend who counseled alcoholic patients told me there is a phenomenon known as Dry Drunk Syndrome. Individuals who are excessive drinkers can exhibit drunken behavior even when not drinking. I worried that this accident was one of those occasions.

I did as Paul asked and went to the police station in Prichard, a suburb of Mobile where the accident had occurred. I was so thankful to learn that Paul was not at fault. He was the victim of a teenage driver on who hit Paul's car around three o'clock in the afternoon when my husband was going to a client's office. The pickup truck the young man was driving veered into the opposite lane of traffic, sideswiped the car in front of Paul, and rammed head-on into Paul's car. Though Paul's wounds were not life threatening, he had very serious leg and foot injuries. The impact pushed the engine into the accelerator; his right foot literally exploded internally. Almost every bone in his foot and ankle was broken, as were two places in his right leg. A left shoulder injury was painful, but minimal.

A week later Paul came home from the hospital, though he was still in a leg cast up to his thigh and in pain from the shoulder injury. It was good to have him home. The medication he took for the pain had an unexpected effect on Paul. One afternoon he insisted that the children and I hop into bed with him as one happy family. The girls looked at their dad and were probably thinking, you're kidding. We did as he asked, though we thought the whole scene was quite silly. I think if he had not had a heavy cast on his leg, I would have watched my husband floating to the ceiling, like Charlie in the Willie Wonka story. The girls and I were laughing the entire time.

After a period of recuperation at home, Paul wore a small lower leg cast, so he could walk with crutches. On the first day out of the house with those crutches, Paul insisted that I accompany him as he walked around the subdivision circle, which probably was at least a half mile. Paul showed his determination to get back to normal. I followed as he painfully exerted all of his effort to make it around the circle. Sweating, puffing, and red-faced, Paul completed the walk. I was so proud of his tenacity and hopeful for a good outcome. However, from then on we both slowly slid from the top of the mountain of hope to the valley of despair.

When a man has lost all happiness, he's not alive. Call him a breathing corpse.

Sophocles
Greek playwright

Paul spent the next six years of his life in and out of hospitals and doctors' offices trying to overcome the effects of at least six operations on his legs and feet. Throughout it all, he continued working as best he could, even when wheelchair bound. We made his office desktop higher by placing bricks under each leg. Every day when he felt able, I drove him to work. I wheeled the chair under his desk, his right leg positioned straight out to support the cast. When he tired, he called me to pick him up.

One of his clients, whose business was in the city of Prichard where Paul was working on the day of the accident, built a ramp for Paul's access to his office. This schedule went on from day-to-day, week-to-week, and month-to-month. It was hard for me to be constantly on call. I did it because I could see no alternative. At this time, Paul would trust no one else to drive him anywhere, even his daughters.

We tried to go out occasionally to dinner and a movie. Each outing was a challenge. Were there stairs to climb? If so, that restaurant was off the list. Could I get the wheelchair up the curb at the nearest movie theater? No. We missed that film. Lifting the wheelchair in and out of the car trunk was another challenge for me. Eventually Paul was strong enough to hobble his way down the passenger side of the car to help me with the lifting. Trying to push 200 plus pounds in a heavy wheelchair was taking its toll on my back muscles.

Working on leather tooling was good therapy. Paul enjoyed making items for personal use, such as a wallet, drink coasters, and a coin purse. To this day, I continue to receive compliments on the etched leather purse he made for me. I thought Paul was on the road to recovery. As it turned out, his recuperation proved that sometimes everything that could go wrong often does.

In 1981 when Paul's mother became ill with terminal lung cancer, it broke my heart to see tears streaming down his face upon learning the awful news. When Paul was mobile enough to attempt a trip to see her, another disaster happened. He developed a bone infection and had to cancel our travel plans. Occasional telephone calls to her gave him no peace of mind. She sounded so sick. He never saw his mother alive again. As in 1960 when his father died, the loss of his parent devastated Paul. This time I accompanied him to his mother's funeral in New York.

It was during these years that my parents moved into our home. Paul was in the hospital at the time. I suppose it was good that I was able to concentrate on the move without having to nurse Paul at home. My folks were no longer able to care for their home and themselves without assistance. Neither was ready for a nursing home. Assisted living facilities and independent senior facilities came later to our community.

My mother died unexpectedly several years later in 1984, leaving me to care for Paul and my elderly father. Paul was angry and frightened. In addition to his physical pain was the financial burden placed upon him. The young driver who caused the accident had no insurance and filed for bankruptcy when he reached age eighteen. The medical expenses totally depleted our insurance coverage. Eventually, we had to spend at least $50,000 of our own resources to cover hospital and other medical bills.

On one hand Paul depended on me to give him the support and help he needed; on the other hand, I was the recipient of his increasing frustration. The nurses at the hospital could not understand why Paul screamed, "Get out!" when I came to see him. Hara told me about a book regarding mental illness titled *I Hate You, Don't Leave Me*, by Jerold J. Kreisman and Hal Strauss. That is exactly how Paul was reacting. I was his personal driver and at-home nurse. Yet, out of his frustration and fear, he projected his anguish onto me.

Paul attempted to work during one month's stay in the hospital. The treatment for a bone infection required his having intravenous antibiotics around the clock through both arms. I brought work papers and a calculator to his hospital room so he could dictate the work to me from his wheelchair. I will never forget one evening when he suddenly stopped dictating and began to bawl like a child. "I'm sure I am going to lose my business," he sobbed. "My clients are going to leave me, I know. I can't work." He was so discouraged at that point, yet still unwilling to seek psychiatric help.

I suppose that is when I began to draw on inner strength by adopting Paul's former sense of humor. At that time, Paul was unwilling to share my vision of what was amusing; he had trouble just coping. I handled the stress by finding humor in some of the most ridiculous experiences we both shared. I still do.

Our daughters coped in different ways. Our younger child immersed herself in school and extracurricular activities. She was away from the house a lot. Hara often holed up in her room, listening to music. She used her art and poetry writing to express her innermost emotions. I discovered one poem Hara wrote after visiting her father in the hospital.

Hospital Lobby

Elevator music is clustered by chatting whispers.
Crutches and canes support bones over there.
Distressed faces sit nervously on puke-green chairs.
Behind head desk hangs an oil portrait of head nurse.

Flowers are the sickness of the day.
To the left, nerve-ending hallway of white tile.
And dark despair reflects death down the aisle.

Here, old women with cat-eyed glasses lay.
Coughs and gags of pain echo down the room,
While the silver spokes of wheelchairs spin by.
An old man lets out an enormous sigh
Of grief and boredom in this ancient tomb.

*Humor is an affirmation of dignity,
a declaration of man's superiority
to all that befalls him.*

> Romain Gary
> French novelist

Paul had two primary doctors treating his injuries from the car wreck. One was an orthopedic surgeon, the other, a plastic surgeon. Both men made extremely early morning hospital rounds. One morning Paul awoke when his plastic surgeon came in with his nurse/assistant. Paul briefly spoke with them, but mostly listened to their conversation as he drifted in and out of slumber. A little later, his other physician entered the room with his nurse. Paul was more alert this time. He chatted with them and told the nurse it was good to see her again. "Mr. Paper, I have not seen you today," she replied. Paul was puzzled. He knew he had heard her voice and seen her in his room earlier; he was insistent. The nurse was equally certain she had not been there earlier. Paul remembered seeing her wedding ring the first time she made rounds. "I am not married. Perhaps you have been dreaming," she told him. When I arrived, he told me what had happened and wondered if the pain medications had caused hallucinations. After all, he was taking some very powerful drugs and Paul was never one to see things. "Barb, I don't understand what is happening to me."

Maybe he was just too sleepy to be fully alert. I knew he was quite upset about this and afraid of the implication that he was losing his senses. It took us awhile to figure out what really was going on. Once we knew, Paul breathed a sigh of relief. I smiled, stifling laughter.

Before Paul's hospitalization, we had not met his plastic surgeon's office nurse. It may have been her day off when we were there. We knew his orthopedic surgeon's nurse from many office visits and previous hospitalizations. She and Paul engaged in friendly banter during their many encounters. We never before knew or even guessed that his doctors had hired identical twin sisters. One sister was married, the other, single

My husband never lost his charm. I wondered how many hospital nurses would bring a pizza to a patient after the evening shift ended at 11:00 because her patient wouldn't eat the hospital food. That's just what one of Paul's nurses did. They later became good friends and she decided to use his accounting services. One never can anticipate how clients can come your way.

Another group of nurses came to visit my husband after his transfer from their hospital to another. Prior to the move, Paul had delighted that nursing staff, in spite of his ranting and raving at me. This group wanted to be sure that Paul received proper care in the new medical facility. Give me a break! Yet, I took all this in stride. It was heartwarming to know that Paul had not lost his gift for gab and ability to entertain. However, he was never able to share my enthusiasm for the humor I found in another hospital episode.

This time Paul was in the hospital for an entire month to treat a foot infection. A primary part of his treatment included daily visits to the rehabilitation department on the first floor where they administered antibiotic footbaths in whirlpool tubs. Transporting my husband from his room to the downstairs facility proved to be a challenge. At least two people, or one very experienced individual, had to help push the wheelchair along with the two IV bags, each attached to an arm on one end and to rolling metal poles on the other. One of my daily visits happened to coincide with his scheduled treatment, so I accompanied him. Little did we know what was in store for us.

We entered a very large tiled room on the first floor, lined with various types of equipment, such as a table for patients, pulleys, and a variety of hand weights. In the center was an enormous steel tub, rather like a small swimming pool. If I did not know I was in a hospital, I would have said I was stumbling upon Dr. Frankenstein's laboratory— menacing.

A very young woman approached us. This technician said, "Mr. Paper, I will be administering your foot treatment." She proceeded to pull out the treatment tub. It was a round metal contraption that reminded me of an old-fashioned washing machine, minus the wringer. Paul found it difficult to lift his injured foot and place it in the tub while sitting in the wheelchair. Several unsuccessful attempts did not help improve his already rancorous disposition.

With Paul's wounded foot finally properly positioned, the young woman poured in some red antiseptic liquid and turned on the water to fill the tub. To do this she had placed a hooked hose in the tub, connected on one end to the faucet on the wall. After a few minutes, we all observed the tub rapidly filling with enormous amounts of bubbles. Moment by moment the bubbles were rising dangerously close to the tub's top rim. After assessing the situation, the technician grabbed a bucket and began bailing out the water as quickly as she could, trying to keep the water level below the flood stage and out of my husband's lap. In went the bucket of water—out went the suds—in went the bucket—out went the suds—again and again. I assumed her goal was to dilute the solution enough to eliminate the rising bubbles. The goal was admirable; success was elusive.

All I could think about while this was going on was the scene of an old *I Love Lucy* television show, when Lucy unsuccessfully tried to keep up with a conveyor belt of candy boxes that she was supposed to be filling. As the belt sped up, Lucy lost control. The young woman with us was losing her control, too. She couldn't bail fast enough. I was chuckling under my breath; Paul was muttering rather loudly, "The water is getting too high!" She cut the water supply, deciding she had put in too much antiseptic.

It was time to empty the tub and try again. She did this with a smaller amount of the red solution. It again began to fill up with water. For a second time, the procedure was in with the bucket, out with the suds, and so on. To our dismay, the bubbles were not any smaller this time and the water level still rapidly rose. I stifled a chuckle, "Turn off the bubble machine." The very distressed young woman tried another bailout. I was again silently laughing, hoping not to upset my husband. Paul was yelling, "Stop, stop, enough!"

At this time, thank goodness, the head of the department walked in and observed what was happening. He suggested that his trainee stop. "Mr. Paper has had enough treatment today."

In my opinion, that was a gigantic understatement. Then the gentleman pointed to the large tub I had spied as we initially entered the room. "That tank is used," he told us, "to treat burn victims. The patient usually is positioned on a large stretcher and bodily lowered into the tub to receive medication. One day a similar mishap took place. A little old lady had been lost among the rising bubbles. They had to hunt for her."

This was not a case of "Tiny Bubbles," the then popular song of Hawaiian singer Don Ho. At this point, we left the lab to return my sullen husband to his room. I could not stop laughing, this time not holding back. Paul did not join my reaction. I believe I recall a few curse words falling from his lips. Perhaps if I had been in his position, my perspective would have been different. I thought what had just happened was funny.

On another occasion Paul was finally able to go back to work on his own. At that time, my husband was again in a leg cast and using crutches, while our energetic younger daughter wore an arm cast, because she was recuperating from broken bones sustained in a cheer leading accident. The week before she had reminded me, "You've never seen my cheerleading squad at a football game." I previously had gone to several basketball games when they performed. Therefore, I said I would come to watch, not knowing what I would end up seeing.

It was a clear fall Friday evening. The football stadium was packed with students, parents, and other interested spectators. I found a seat in the bleachers where I could watch my daughter's cheerleading squad, but never made it past the first quarter of the game. I saw my child standing on her partner's shoulders as they shouted out a cheer. The next thing I saw was her body tilting backward. Her partner held on to my daughter's feet to keep her from falling. That was the wrong thing to do. Trying to prevent landing on her back, she stretched out her arms to brace herself. Her right arm broke in several places. That night every football player knocking into one another during the game came away in one piece, but not our daughter. There I was, on my way to an emergency room again, this time with my wounded child. I detected a pattern developing.

On the following Monday morning, she and Paul were leaving the house together on their way to school and work—arm cast and leg cast in place. I envisioned the "Spirit of 76" marching out. All that were missing were the eye-patched fife and drum players.

That's the thing about depression
The fog is like a cage without a key.

Elizabeth Wurtzel
Author/actor

By 1985, Paul's condition had slowly deteriorated. He had begun smoking again while in the hospital. "I've been so nervous I got someone to get a pack of cigarettes for me," he said. His habit of overeating and not exercising caused more weight gain. In contrast to the first years of our marriage when he couldn't wait to arrive home to me, now it seemed to me that he was always leaving. I still remember the emptiness and disappointment I felt each time he physically moved farther and farther away from me. I hated to hear the sound of the closing door as he left each day. He was turning away emotionally as well. His business stresses weighed heavily on him and his foot caused him constant pain.

One day he wanted just the two of us to go out to dinner. It was an important evening for me, because we had not gone out together without the family in a very long time. While waiting for our food to arrive, Paul said, "Barbara, there is something I have to discuss with you." From his serious tone of voice, I could tell it was not going to be good.

"Paul, please, can you tell me later at home? I really want to enjoy our dinner together."

"If you don't want to hear what I have to say now, then you don't need to know."

I never found out what he wanted to tell me. I didn't enjoy the evening, after all. I should have recognized and resisted his attempt to be controlling.

On June 19, 1985, we celebrated our twenty-fifth wedding anniversary. Our girls bought a special cake decorated with intertwined wedding rings and put up some home decorations to celebrate the occasion. Paul and I kissed for a photo. I used my smile to pretend that all was well with us, that he loved me as in the beginning. From time to time, I look at that photo and think that perhaps Paul was also trying to recapture what we had, but his forced smile belied the reality.

Often people with depression have chronic pain or other physical problems that do not respond to treatment. By the end of 1985, Paul was crippled, having lost part of his foot to gangrene and a section of his leg for a bone graft. He had to have a special shoe with a lift and needed a cane to help him walk. Each morning I watched him rub his damaged foot, trying to ease the constant pain before attempting to put on his orthopedic shoe. He was aware he could no longer do the former activities that were his pleasure, such as bowling and dancing.

Paul was so dejected. He struggled with his daily routine and had little to say to me. I never suspected that he would agree to accompany me on a week's trip to the Catskill Mountains for a professional conference of administrators for a non-profit organization, a position I took several years before. The resort was old, probably beautiful during its heyday. There were older couples there not associated with the conference. It was reminiscent of the resort in the film, *Dirty Dancing*. This was my first trip to upstate New York. I attended daytime meetings. Paul joined me for lunches and in the evenings, for meals and entertainment.

It seemed to me he enjoyed being away from his daily routine and was able to genuinely relax. He did not drink much during that week. For that, I was grateful and relaxed, too. One evening the hotel provided after dinner dance music.

Paul offered me his hand as he led me up a few steps to the dance floor. A feeling of happy nostalgia swept over me. Paul tried the dance moves we had done so many times before. His rhythm was not the same. He couldn't maneuver his feet. I did most of the moving while he helped me turn. I held him tightly, not wanting him to know how sad it made me feel, not wanting to let him go. From a condolence letter I received after his death, I learned that during that week he had talked with one of my male colleagues about their mutual concerns regarding diets, work habits, and cholesterol levels. Paul then realized that he had to take control of himself before it was too late.

SAN FRANCISCO, CALIFORNIA

A trip to San Francisco during the year before he died in 1986, granted us a brief respite and last good time together. We had won a raffle that awarded us round trip airline tickets to anywhere in the continental United States. I chose San Francisco. Paul was behaving like a grouchy bear on the day we were to leave. He fussed and complained. I watched an amazing transformation as the plane took off. At departure, Paul was tense and obviously preoccupied. Yet, the farther away the plane flew from Mobile, the more Paul's face relaxed. There was a complete metamorphosis. By the time we arrived, he was looking forward to the days ahead.

This was a wonderful time. Even though Paul was in pain, we managed to take in the sights, see a stage show, have marvelous meals, enjoy Columbus Day at an Italian celebration in one of the bayside enclosed wharves, go to the zoo, and attend our first comedy club performance. I think we were the oldest couple in the club; we didn't care. It was special for us to be laughing together again.

The only time he really complained was the day we took the ferry to Sausalito. Trying to maneuver the hilly streets proved too much for him. "I'm going to stop at this bar and rest," he said. "My foot is hurting. You go on and give me some time alone." I know he took several drinks while he rested. When I came back, he was ready to resume our sightseeing on level ground. I treasure the memories of that trip. He never was out of control. However, every photograph I took of Paul shows him sullen, pensive, and sad. Perhaps he suspected what was to come.

My only fear is that I may live too long. This would be a subject of dread to me.

Thomas Jefferson

MOBILE, ALABAMA

After the trip, Paul's demeanor gradually became more depressed and despondent. Previously, when Paul was in his up mood, I marveled at his sense of humor. I realized that Paul was in serious trouble toward the end of his too short life when he found absolutely no reason to laugh. He rebuffed my attempts to encourage him. "Paul, I want to grow old with you." His response was, "Barbara, I don't want to grow old." He firmly believed he would die young, like his father. Paul's general health was gradually deteriorating. It seemed that Paul's body was increasingly becoming tolerant of the alcohol. As Paul continued his excessive drinking, he was causing more damage to his body, relationships, finances, and work.

For over a month Paul slaved to recreate a client's missing file. He had frantically searched everywhere. He even accused a former employee of taking it. I honestly don't know what happened because Paul never had lost or misplaced his work in all of the years he had his accounting practice. I had no choice but to allow him to deal with this crisis as he saw fit. He would not have taken my advice at this time anyway.

I thought all of this turmoil was enough until it became more difficult for Paul to perform sexually. I suspect he was having vascular problems along with his excessive smoking, drinking, and weight gain. Once he offhandedly told me he would get a penal implant and that he was going to enroll in a pain management program. "Paul, that's good," I told him. He never did either one.

One evening while driving us to dinner, my frustration peaked and I began to cry. "Paul, please go to a doctor. Get a checkup," I pleaded. The sound of my voice became louder, as I almost screamed at him, "I have been with you through all of your problems. It isn't fair. I am a normal woman." Paul looked at me with disdain and said, "Go f*** yourself or get a lover and don't tell me about it." Stunned, I drove on without a word. What could I possibly say? He had never spoken such ugly words to me. Where was the man who professed his undying love? I knew in my heart that Paul did not mean those hurtful words. Yet, I was so upset and angry that he did not have the courage at that point to do something so important for me or for us. Today I turn on the television and watch ads for various remedies for ED. In the eighties, no one would have uttered the words, erectile dysfunction, aloud. Times have certainly changed.

Breathing problems caused him to snore louder than normal, something I could not endure. It kept me from getting the rest I needed. I had no choice but to sleep in another bedroom. He didn't understand. At that time, I had never heard of sleep apnea, a condition when the sleeper repeatedly stops breathing throughout the night; loud snoring is one symptom. Our elder daughter was recently diagnosed with sleep apnea.

One evening when I was leaving his bedside after saying good night, he gripped my hand. "Paul, you're hurting me," I said, almost in tears. I tried to pull away, but he wouldn't let go. Finally, he released his grip; I left the room. I cried myself to sleep that and many other evenings. Paul was in serious trouble and I did not know how to help him.

Not long after, he drove alone to Birmingham for a weekend accounting seminar, a yearly requirement for maintaining his professional certification. Upon his return he told me, "One night I went to the hotel bar where there was a pianist. I got up in front of the crowd and sang." He didn't have to tell me the name of the song. I knew it had to be "Fly Me to the Moon," his favorite song. "They really liked me." he exclaimed. After all these years, Paul still could not accept his magnetism and worth. From then on, I rarely saw him. He would get up, get dressed, leave for the day, and return late in the evening to sleep. He was never in a mood to converse with any family member.

Months before, Paul and I had made plans to go on a trip to New Orleans for a weekend. He won the hotel accommodations at another fundraiser. In one of his quarrelsome moods as he was arising from bed, Paul announced to me, "Cancel the trip; we're not going." I did not understand.

"Paul, we have the reservations."

"I don't want to go. I'm too busy."

"It will be a nice getaway, please let's go."

"Cancel the reservations."

"We've planned this trip for a while. You're not making any sense."

None of my arguments persuaded him to change his mind. It was at this point that I made a decision I never thought I could make. I was going to take the trip alone; I was not going to give in to his arbitrary pronouncements any longer. I suppose this was my declaration of independence—it was my awakening. I had to take control of my life and not depend on my husband. I hoped he would come with me after all. I left a note for Paul indicating the time when I was leaving. I packed my bags, told my family where I was going, and drove off alone. I was angry, scared, and determined. I felt as if I were being pulled into an emotional whirlpool that would take me down with Paul. I was not going to let that happen.

My New Orleans escape was not enjoyable. After parking my car in the hotel's garage, I walked into the Hotel Monteleone, an old, but elegant New Orleans landmark. As the desk clerk was checking me in, I glanced around the lobby and high ceiling. I recalled a similar check-in with my parents when I was around eleven years old, impressed by the luxurious surroundings. It had not changed through all the passing years, though I am sure renovations had taken place. No doubt those walls surrounded travelers from around the world and reverberated with the sounds of many languages interspersed with the local Cajun dialects. Two favorite Cajun words I enjoyed using are beignet (ben-yea), the wonderful French Market doughnut and lagniappe (lan-yap), a little something extra.

During the daytime, I shopped and walked around the French Quarter. Knowing it was unsafe for a woman to wander alone at night, I ate dinner at the hotel snack shop and watched TV in my room. It was quite disconcerting to look at myself alone reflected in the mirrored bed canopy. What a waste of a romantic retreat.

Later I spoke to Paul about my trip. He told me, "I read the note. Barbara, I thought you didn't want me to come. So, I didn't." That is when the discrepancy between what I expected to happen and his irrational thinking became apparent. I thought he would decide to come with me.

The lesson learned was that at some point when dealing with a person who is suffering from mental illness, the enabler has to disengage from the situation. It is very easy to lose one's self-esteem. It takes strength and determination to disconnect and try to be objective. After all is said and done, the ill person needs emotionless support, even though it isn't easy.

The Chanuka holiday, the Jewish Festival of Lights, began the week after my New Orleans trip. Paul must have been frightened by my independent actions. I had never done anything like that before. "I thought you were going to leave me," he said as he handed me a big gift box. Inside was a lovely mink jacket.

"Paul, this is beautiful."

"Try it on."

"It fits perfectly. How do I look?"

"Great!"

I wondered if I should ask if we could afford this. Foolishly, I put my doubts aside and allowed Paul to manipulate me. I was again enabling his destructive behavior. I had not stepped back and thought rationally regarding his action. After Paul died, I unsuccessfully tried to return the coat, and ended up having to pay for it myself.

INTERSTATE HIGHWAY 10

During the summer of 1985, we drove our daughter, Hara, to New Orleans to take a flight to visit a college friend. Paul and I left the airport to drive home after seeing her off. That is when the downpour began. The persistent rain came down making it difficult for drivers to see. Some cars passed us; others cautiously drove through the unrelenting rain. Paul was driving over the speed limit through the blinding downpour, even though other drivers were parking on the side of the road. "Paul, slow down. Let's pull over and wait until it clears up. We aren't in a hurry." I could have been speaking to myself. He refused to respond to my pleas or slow down; it was as if I were not there; my words were bouncing off deaf ears. He persisted no matter what the consequences. Paul had an angry, determined look on his face. There was neither a deadline nor any rational reason for his behavior.

The car trip on Interstate 10 normally takes just a few hours. This time I wished it had taken longer. I was thankful we arrived home unhurt. Paul's behavior was totally irrational. As far as I knew, he had not been drinking. His behavior was not like that of the man I married. I truly did not know what to do at this point.

In May of 1986, he and our younger daughter attended the college graduation of Paul's nephew in Atlanta. I chose not to go. I wanted her to have some one-on-one time with her dad. I could no longer endure being around Paul without wanting to cry. It was painful to watch his physical and emotional deterioration. I later learned that Paul presented his nephew with his most prized possession, his pinky ring. Paul never took that ring off his finger. It had been his father's ring and meant the world to him as a loving reminder of his dad. I thought Paul would never part with it. In retrospect, perhaps he was sending a message.

Not long after that trip was the final push into the abyss of complete despair. Paul lost a client who accounted for thirty percent of our annual income. There seemed to be no rational explanation for Paul's losing the account, because he had recently and successfully represented the man's business in tax court, saving the company a lot of money. One day Paul told me, "I hate my job. I wish we could have moved to Phoenix, Arizona, like I wanted to do after school."

"Paul, I will do whatever you want. If you want to move to Phoenix, I will. My father told me he would go anywhere I wanted to be."

"No, it's too late."

"Honey, it's never too late."

Before our marriage, Paul spoke about wanting to go to Phoenix. I never took it seriously because we knew nobody there and he had a job waiting in Mobile where my family lived. At the time, it seemed an impossible move for me. I suppose I was afraid to move so far away from my family and familiar surroundings. Now, no matter how I tried, I couldn't convince Paul that moving was something we could do. I would have done anything to have a normal happy life with my family.

Because I could not stop for Death,
He kindly stopped for me.

Emily Dickinson
Poet

Believe it or not, we laughed at Paul's funeral. Why? I suppose I must take full responsibility. When the rabbi who was to lead the graveside services asked me about Paul, I tried to explain about Paul's unusual sense of humor. The rabbi was new to our congregation and had not had the opportunity to know my husband personally. Paul had often told me that when the time came, not to bury him with a traditional funeral. His instructions were, "Take my body downtown to Fort Conde and shoot me out of the cannon into Mobile Bay." I had no warning that the rabbi would share those instructions with the graveside mourners. We all had the image of what Paul wanted etched in our psyches forever. We could not help ourselves; we laughed. Pinny/Paul would have been pleased.

I received a number of touching letters from Paul's acquaintances and business associates. One significant letter from a client reveals so much about Paul's personality. He wrote, "I remember Paul when he first came into our office, fresh out of the university, and how he developed so quickly into a close friend as well as a business associate. He was the life of our Christman (sic) parties and our staff always looked forward to his dry wit. There were few better read and knowledgeable on world affairs, and it was a pleasure to discuss a whole range of subjects with him whenever our paths crossed at lunch or in our offices."

After Paul's death, my children and I considered arranging to have one of his special witticisms etched in his gravestone. He found as many occasions as possible to use it during his lifetime. When he was leaving their homes Paul would tease party hosts, who were not easily offended friends, by saying, "I had a good time, but this isn't it." As apropos as the sentence may have been for describing Paul's outlook on life, future cemetery visitors might have found this sentiment rather perplexing. Therefore, my daughters and I agreed we would instead choose a quote from the poet Keats. Paul loved this phrase and posted it in his office. He often used it in conversations. We believed it exemplified the essence of Paul's true character and soul, "A thing of beauty is a joy forever."

*There can be no deep disappointment
where there is not deep love.*

> Martin Luther King, Jr.
> Civil rights leader/minister

Because my husband was a certified public accountant, I assumed he was good at handling money. I never questioned him about this, even though there were occasions when he didn't pay our utility bills in a timely fashion. Once the gas company cut off our home service due to his negligence. Paul always had an excuse/reason for what happened. I continued to let him control our family's finances. What a gigantic mistake. I did not understand that excessive spending was symptomatic of some mental illnesses. If he told me that we could afford something, I believed him. I wanted to believe him. I was in total denial of my own capacity to take hold of the situation. I convinced myself that I needed Paul to take care of us, i.e., my codependency.

When he died, I was shocked to find I did not have enough money in our checking account to pay for my daughter's airplane ticket from college in Sarasota, Florida. I had to borrow money for food for that week. Not only were there no immediate funds available, but Paul's estate was insolvent. I later learned that he had credit card debts of over $50,000, primarily bar bills on credit cards in his name only. This man had said he lived to do for me. I am convinced now that he died to do for me. Hara told me that someone at the Bombay Bicycle Club, one of his frequent hangouts, placed Paul's picture in the front window. I didn't know if I should have been honored or embarrassed. I never saw that photo, nor did I want to see it.

Two weeks before his death, Paul had applied for additional life insurance. I received a telephone call from the insurers to schedule a medical screening for Paul in connection with his application. Of course, I told the caller he had passed away. I dismissed it from my mind. However, miracle of miracles, because the company had accepted his initial check, they honored the application. I received the additional insurance check along with the insurance money already sent to me. Paul's death made it possible for my daughters and me to survive. Paul allowed nature to take its course without his intervention to fulfill his death wish. In my heart, I know this was his lasting act of love, in spite of his troubled mind. If he had committed overt suicide, the life insurance policy would have been null and void.

About a year after he died, I was at home doing some housekeeping. The doorbell rang to announce a most unexpected visitor, Paul's friend who had found him on his deathbed. I was surprised. I directed him to the study in the back of the house so we could have a private conversation away from my father.

Bobby explained, "I have been away from Mobile at an alcoholics' rehabilitation center. My friends finally convinced me to go." It seems that he was so stricken by Paul's death that he continued to abuse alcohol even more than before. Bobby was obviously inebriated at Paul's funeral. "I have been sober for many months now and plan to marry," he told me. Part of his rehabilitation was to make peace with individuals whom he may have harmed. We spoke about Paul and their many evenings together drinking and convincing each other that they were buddies against the world. He assured me that I probably would have had no influence on Paul just before he died. In some way, it made me feel better to know that, though I still have feelings of guilt that I was unable to convince Paul to get the help he needed. Even today, I wonder if I could have done more for him. I will never know.

I have learned a lot about mental illness since Paul's death. An article from the School of Medicine at Washington University in St. Louis, MO, has identified a gene linking alcoholism and depression. The article also said that often, as in Paul's case, alcohol dependence could remain undetected for years. Our daughter's battle to overcome her own demons demanded that I learn more in order to help her. I have learned that 50 percent of all lifetime cases of mental illness begin by the age of 14 and 75 percent, by age 24.

I know the best of Paul survives in his daughters. I miss the man I married and the man I believe he was supposed to be if he had not been ill. Our oldest daughter continues to exhibit her quick wit and sense of humor, among her many wonderful artistic qualities. Her sister, besides being very intelligent and lovely, constantly demonstrates her love and appreciation of family, as her father once did, devoting many volunteer hours at her children's school, scheduling family outings, and supporting all of her boys' activities and challenges.

A plant is like a self-willed man, out of whom we can obtain all which we desire, if we will only treat him his own way.

Johann Wolfgang von Goethe
Writer/artist

I took home all of the plants from Paul's office that looked as if they would survive; only one made it. I was so pleased several years later in 1990, after I had moved to Atlanta, GA, to discover the one plant had unusual pink flowers bursting open to display additional pink splendor. It was as if one flower gave birth to another. I had never seen anything like that.

In 2001, I had a battle with a colony of mealy bugs. These little creatures love to munch on plants and eventually cause their demise. I tried everything from spraying the plant with lethal insecticides to applying alcohol with Q-tips in an attempt to destroy each patch of bugs, one-by-one. My last effort was to wipe each leaf and stem supporting the dreaded enemy as they continually reappeared. One might ask, "Why were you bothering to challenge these bugs?"

This was Paul's plant, his pride and joy. I am not sure of its botanical name. To me it was just Paul's plant. He nurtured it from infancy until it grew to full beauty. Then he lovingly placed it on a glass shelf in the only window in his office. The light was perfect for flourishing greenery. All of his plants were beautiful. For some reason he treasured this one most of all. However, when the mealy army attacked, I was trying so hard to save it. If I were unsuccessful, it would be as if I had lost Paul again.

Boxing CA 1950

Sucking it in

Jason's Jamboree 1957
(Photo courtesy of The W.S. Hole Special
Collections Library, the
University of Alabama)

Happily engaged

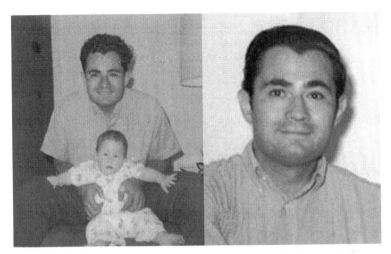

Paul and Hara 1964   Looking good in 1967

Paul clowning around 1972   25th wedding anniversary

"Don't take my picture!"

San Francisco 1985

Humanity can be quite cold to those whose eyes see the world differently.

>Eric A. Burns
>Author

MOBILE, ALABAMA

Hara's problems began in her preteen years; however, she had been showing signs of a disorder much earlier. When she was approximately four years old, she had difficulty adjusting to large crowds of people. Often I would have to remove her from birthday parties when she began screaming. Small gatherings did not bother her as much. Even today, as an adult, she is uncomfortable at large social gatherings.

It was hard to watch my precious, talented, and intelligent child, born with red hair and a sweet disposition, emerge into a personality I hardly recognized. Throughout her early years, she was so easy to manage. While I cooked and cleaned, she was contented sitting on the kitchen floor with an assortment of pots, pans, and spoons to keep her occupied.

I recognized her artistic talents when she was about three years old, and encouraged her creativity. When she reached eight years old, she asked for guitar lessons. Paul and I decided to go the serious route. We bought her a proper classical guitar and hired a qualified instructor. Hara loved her music then, as she does to this day, when she is able to perform her own music and lyrics to appreciative audiences. She is a skilled musician.

Hara excelled in her studies at a private school with small classes from pre-kindergarten through fifth grade. Difficulties adjusting became more apparent when she began sixth grade in a new public middle school. Our daughter struggled socially through middle and high school classes. When she was thirteen, I took her to a psychologist for routine testing. The results showed that she had an extraordinarily high score in nonverbal skills, such as math, art, and music. He told me he had never had anyone score so high. However, trying to express herself verbally was a challenge for her as a youth and today as an adult.

She was a loner with no real friends. Her artistic talents were her entrée into minimal acceptance by her peers. **During her middle school years, she spent many hours wandering the neighborhood. She was a lost soul. One evening my husband and I received a telephone call, the kind no parent wants to receive. I picked up the phone to answer a ring.

"Hello."

"Is this Mrs. Paper?"

"Yes, it is."

"Do you have a teenage daughter?"

"Why do you ask?"

"You need to come to K-mart; she has been caught shoplifting."

The person on the other end did not have to tell me which daughter they were describing, I knew it was Hara. The store was within walking distance of our home. Paul went and tried to settle the matter. Unfortunately, he had to go to the police station to get her.

The juvenile court put her on probation and eventually closed the record. It is not surprising that someone in her state of mind would push the limit either to get attention or find some excitement in her life. Stealing was out of character for my child who knew right from wrong. She had never before been in any trouble of her own doing. We were more distressed than angry. This kind of behavior may stem from a teenager's sense of loneliness. At the time I read somewhere that one-third of those caught shoplifting were suffering from depression. High school was another challenging time for Hara.

Her younger sister was very popular and had many friends; Hara did not. Even though she participated in art and music activities and was in advanced classes, Hara couldn't connect with her peers. Young people can be terribly cruel to one who is different; she was subjected daily to name-calling such as 'Hara the horror' or 'toilet paper', as well as physical and emotional harassment, such as pushing her, putting tacks on the seat of her chair, and spitting on her artwork. Whenever one of her drawings or paintings was placed on display, someone stole it.

At the high school senior class annual so-called awards program, the senior named most likely to be an old maid was Hara. This would be a terrible insult to any young person. To someone with low self-esteem, it was unspeakably cruel. Today we call it bullying. So much had happened during her formative years to intensify her problems.

Our daughter went her own way alone. At home, there were displays of her anger and frustration. Twice Hara put her hands through the glass in our French doors, once needing stitches. She also punched the wall hard enough to cause a hole. I've learned that depression also brings on sadness, feelings of worthlessness or guilt which don't go away. It is often difficult to know if a teenager is simply having growing up pains or is really mentally ill. I had no doubt about my child's condition. No one should be totally friendless.

Attempts to bring her out socially through sleep-away camps and out-of-town learning trips with other high school students were fruitless. She just could not connect. A friend of mine who had guided one trip told me, "Your daughter was apart from the others. She just wasn't making friends." We all knew something was wrong, but didn't know how to fix it.

While in high school, she began working at McDonald's to earn some extra spending money. A male customer she served showed an interest in her. Of course, she was flattered and so desperate to find a boyfriend.

One evening she foolishly went with him to his apartment. The cruelty of being called an old maid took more of a toll on her than I realized. Loneliness compounded by depression often leads to risky behavior. This visit became more than risky. Later that evening I heard her crying while softly walking down the hallway at home. I got up from bed and saw her wearing disheveled clothes. "Honey, what happened?" "Mom, I was raped." I listened as she explained. "He told me he wanted me to see the new furniture he bought for his apartment, but I knew something was not right as soon as I walked in and saw no furniture. I told him no when he started feeling and kissing me, but he wouldn't let me leave."

"Why in the world did you go to his apartment?"

"Mom, I—I don't know."

Once he was finished with her, she left as quickly as she could and came home.

After high school graduation, she attended the University of South Alabama in Mobile, with a music grant to play in the classical guitar ensemble. It soon became apparent to her that she really did not want to be a professional musician. During this period she would, as her father had done before, leave for solo evenings out, not returning until late hours. I did not know where she was or whom she was with. I was reliving all of the trepidation and worry that I had with her dad. Each time I was grateful to hear her car door close and the turn of the key in the back door lock. Then I could fall asleep.

Because she wanted more independence and we wanted her to accept responsibility for herself, she moved into a dorm room on campus. The person in charge of housing first placed her with a senior who was constantly sexually entertaining male friends and always playing loud music. This situation caused our daughter a lot of stress. I spoke with the housing administrator who reassigned Hara to a four-student apartment with three girls who also made her life miserable. She didn't know how to relate to these girls, either. The administration eventually expelled them for drug use, leaving Hara alone in the apartment for about six weeks. Hara put many of her favorite posters on the walls of the unit to make it seem more like her bedroom at home.

Then two new girls were assigned to the unit. They arrived before our daughter even had a chance to meet them. Upon returning to the apartment after classes, Hara discovered that the girls had removed all of her posters, ripped them up, thrown them on her bed, and redecorated the walls to their liking. She told me the girls repeatedly had parties in the apartment and used her portable stereo without permission, even taking it out of the unit at times. Hara chained and locked her stereo to a cabinet.

She and I made a formal complaint to the university's housing administrator regarding the poor choice of roommates and their unacceptable behavior. The administrator was uncooperative at our meeting and unable to provide a workable solution to Hara's housing dilemma. After a thorough discussion, Paul and I decided to move our daughter to an off-campus apartment nearby where she could live alone and continue her studies without distraction. This arrangement worked well; her grades improved.

Since she decided not pursue a career in music, Paul and I encouraged her to pursue her artistic talents, which led Hara to apply to the Ringling School of Art and Design in Sarasota. Paul took the time to drive her to Florida with her art portfolio for a personal interview with the admission officer. The trip was a vacation for both of them. He and I were proud to learn of her acceptance.

SARASOTA, FLORIDA

After she arrived in Sarasota, again she had a difficult time adjusting. There were periodic telephone calls to me to talk about her struggles and stresses. She never asked to speak to her dad. In 1986, during her second year of studies, Paul passed away and her problems grew exponentially. Hara wanted to quit college, but I convinced her to continue because her dad would have liked to see her graduate and I thought it was important.

Like her father, she used unconventional self-medication. At one point, she admitted herself to get treatment at a psychiatric hospital, the Bayside Center for Behavioral Health, part of the Sarasota Memorial Hospital System. Despite her struggles and an unhappy love affair, she graduated with a BA Degree in Illustration.

It was a bittersweet time when I attended her graduation alone. I flew to Sarasota for the occasion. My dad, who was living with me, was physically unable to make the trip and her sister was in the middle of college final exams. The commencement ceremony was to take place at the symphony hall in Sarasota. The seashell shaped theater roof was beautiful. The exterior and interior colors were striking shades of purples and lavenders. The color tones were peaceful, but I had to fight back the tears as my child accepted her diploma. I had never felt so alone. As she was walking to the stage I thought, Paul would have been as proud as I am.

Hara and I took time in Sarasota to enjoy some of the sights and eat wonderful seafood. Then we packed up her belongings and towed a small trailer back home to Mobile. After a few days, I said to her, "You have a month at home to do what you want. Then I want you to find a job." At the end of the month, she left for a week in Atlanta, GA, and returned with a job, an apartment, and a roommate waiting for her. I was proud of her independence and hoped it was a new beginning for her. We said our good-byes; then she drove away to a new life. I prayed this would be a positive turning point for her.

Hope is the thing with feathers
That perches in the soul,
And sings the tune without the words,
And never stops at all.

Emily Dickinson
Poet

ATLANTA, GEORGIA

In the 1990s, Hara and I were living in Atlanta. I had moved from Mobile after my father died in 1989. My older daughter went through periods of normalcy alternating with severe depression. After a brief and unhappy marriage in 1989, ending in divorce, Hara's pattern of stress followed by debilitating depression became more pronounced. She kept having unsuccessful romantic relationships. Each time she was attracted to men who were unstable and ultimately disappointed her. Attempts to find a therapist who could help her were generally unsuccessful. Various doctors at the Emory University Clinic and elsewhere prescribed a variety of mood-altering drugs, trying to find the right combination.

At one time, her symptoms from over-dosage of a potent prescription, Topamax, frightened us. Hara called it stupamax after having a bad reaction to this medication. On weekend evenings, Hara worked for extra income at a hotdog stand in a popular Atlanta bar strip. One night before the end of her shift, she experienced unsteadiness and slurred speech. Someone at work drove her home. She managed to call me and by the time I arrived at her place, she could not speak at all and could not sit still. A trip to the closest emergency room at Gwinnett Medical Center was necessary to get her back on a proper track. We waited for the emergency room doctor to give us an encouraging word. I was worrying. Would she be okay?

Trying to find the correct combination and dosages of the many drugs available for depression, called a prescription cocktail, was one of the challenges she faced. This time the combination had been wrong. Thank goodness, she was going to be all right. Finding another therapist with whom she could feel comfortable was challenging. It took perseverance to locate the right doctor for her treatment. After she found a new therapist, Hara wasn't able to return to work until she adjusted to the new medications prescribed for her personality disorder (BPD) along with being bipolar, experiencing SAD (seasonal affective disorder) and ADD (attention deficit disorder). I have no doubt in my mind that this was Paul's undiagnosed illness.

I concluded that her condition was not serious, just borderline. The opposite is true; patients with BPD may suffer from many different disorders. The borderline term refers to the fact that it may border on very serious mental illnesses with many different troublesome symptoms. It is one of the most difficult conditions to diagnose and treat. It was not until the 1980s that BPD was recognized as a separate diagnosis.

Before I began writing this memoir, I did more research regarding mental illness. As previously stated, there are many detailed descriptions of the causes and symptoms of BPD, which are difficult to diagnose and often associated with bipolar disorder. A person with unipolar depression may endure the same mood for weeks or months; however, a person with borderline personality disorder may experience intense bouts of anger, depression, and anxiety lasting only hours, or at most a day. Paul told me he often felt he was sitting on his shoulder watching himself. Hara told me of observing herself in the same way, as if she were detached from her body. That is the tragedy of mental illness. The path to normalcy has many wrong turns.

After Hara's job took her to Raleigh, North Carolina, I tried to visit my daughter as often as I could and as often as she wanted me there. Some visits were stressful. I honed my ducking skills. Once in anger and frustration, she hurled a desk stapler at me. Of course, Hara apologized later when she was calm and more in control.

What may seem like ordinary inconveniences or obstacles to an average person can seem insurmountable to someone who is bipolar or has borderline personality disorder. This cycle of semi-stability followed by short periods of disability continued for at least a year. With the help of a new therapist in Durham, NC, she began to attend a group program, Dialectic Behavior Therapy (DBT), to help develop coping skills. I was grateful that she was trying to take care of herself.

Children are a great comfort in your old age and they help you reach it faster, too.

Lionel Kauffman
Author

So much has happened in my daughter's life that duplicates my husband's travails. I was at my apartment one evening near bedtime when the telephone rang. It was long-distance from my troubled daughter.

"Mom, I've called to say good-bye."

"Honey, what's wrong?"

"I can't take it anymore. I'm hurting."

She was so depressed she wanted to end it all. The physical agony she was experiencing made her feel worse.

Ten percent of people struggling with borderline personality disorder commit suicide, particularly females. This rate is more than fifty times the rate of suicide in the general population. I did not want my daughter to be a statistic. I had lost Paul, my first *Moon Flyer*. I feared Hara would fly away, too. It was 2001. I was in Atlanta; she was miles away. What could I do? I telephoned her therapist in Raleigh. It was lucky that I reached her. Perhaps someone was still watching over my child. I told the psychologist,

"I just received a call; Hara sounded desperate. I think she wants to kill herself." Her therapist responded, "I will call the Raleigh Police Department to send officers to take her to Holly Hill Hospital. I'll contact the hospital so the physician in charge will expect her."

"Thank you. I am going to drive to Raleigh right away. Please keep in touch so I'll know what's happening."

The Raleigh police arrived in time and convinced my daughter to go with them to the hospital for a psychiatric evaluation. I packed my clothes, filled the gas tank in my car, and left Atlanta right away. That was a dreadful seven-hour trip, not knowing exactly what I would find when I arrived.

I found her stressed and withdrawn, but willing to take advantage of the treatment. Two days in the hospital were enough. She was all right for now. One of the factors that led to her despair was her monthly menstrual cycles. The depression increased tremendously during her periods when she experienced extreme physical pain. A family friend who is a physician informed us that Lupron injections were available to prematurely stop the menstrual cycle. The injections tricked her body into thinking she was experiencing menopause, but they were only a temporary solution. The monthly injections could be taken for no longer than eighteen months without serious side effects.

It was eventually necessary for her to have a hysterectomy in 2003. This surgery often brings a sense of loss to many women, but it was obvious she would never be able to care for a child. I was sad that she could never experience motherhood, but also relieved that she would no longer have to suffer monthly. Her Raleigh therapist and I agreed that my daughter was no longer able to live so far from family. It was important that she leave

Raleigh and come closer to me. The solution was that she move to Chattanooga, Tennessee, where my son-in-law's family lived. They were willing to help her make that transition. I knew the change was necessary, but worried about the ordeal of moving.

Murphy's Law is an observation that anything that can go wrong, will go wrong.

>   Edward A. Murphy
>   Engineer

The adventure began in April 2002 as I prepared to go to Raleigh to help Hara move to her new apartment in Ringgold, Georgia, a community adjacent to Chattanooga. The plans were rather routine—first reserve a rental truck for the move, fly to Raleigh to help her pack her belongings, and travel in her car to the new location. How naive I was to believe the adventure would be a routine trip. My life had thus far been nothing resembling routine. What I am now relating is the truth as it happened. Murphy was somehow with us as an uninvited traveler. I recall it all with amusement.

With all that has occurred since 9/11, I assumed that a one-way airline ticket to Raleigh would be the red flag allowing me the privilege of being screened, searched, and patted down as I made my way through the stages of the Atlanta airport security. I wasn't wrong and met this challenge without undue stress or delay. Everything was on schedule. I arrived at the Raleigh airport where my daughter picked me up.

She had always been a collector, in other words, a pack rat. We decided that having a garage sale would help reduce the amount of stuff to transport. She and I were rather good at the garage sale business. We had perfected a system of sorting, gathering, advertising, and selling which would put any used car salesman to shame. The sale was a success; yet somehow she still had a lot of stuff.

We were ready to tackle the main task at hand, packing. My daughter had some boxes left from a previous move, but certainly not enough to properly protect her current belongings.

"Honey, where do you want to get more packing supplies?"

"Mom, it costs too much to buy them. I have an idea.

"What is it?"

"Let's check out the dumpsters behind stores. I'll bet they have boxes we can use."

I don't know why I let her talk me into doing that. It was messy after an overnight rain. Once we finished gathering the boxes and packing materials, we took much needed showers and afternoon naps. Then we were ready to get started.

While all of this was going on, my daughter's menagerie of pets endured the indignity of having their home dismantled. My three grandkitties, Apollo, Atlas, and Eros, found hiding places or just scampered out of our way while we packed, shoved, and rearranged the furniture. There were two unnamed gerbils also living in a multilevel habitat in which any self-respecting gerbil would happily stay.

We later discovered that one adventurous gerbil had found an escape route and ventured out to explore the big wide world of the bedroom. Hara was certain she knew where the little adventurer was hiding; this was not his first escape. We searched all over the apartment to no avail. Where could he be?

Lo and behold, I saw the rodent's head sticking out of the space in her treadmill motor. The little guy just wouldn't come out and retreated to an enclosed area of the motor compartment. We tried everything we could to coax him out of his hiding place. First we made banging noises on the treadmill frame—no luck. Next, we tried shaking the very heavy machine. Finally, we tried running the vacuum cleaner close to the assembly, hoping he would run out in terror. The miniature daredevil didn't fall for that trick. The most we accomplished was leaving a strip of fairly clean bedroom carpet. There was only one alternative. Armed with a screwdriver, my daughter disassembled the motor section. There he was. She grabbed him and put the reluctant tenant back where he belonged.

While I was in Raleigh, my daughter slept in her bedroom with her caged noisy gerbils. I am a light sleeper and couldn't have gotten my rest with their shenanigans. Therefore, I camped out on a pumped up air mattress in the office/bedroom. There were a few times when I suspected a slight leakage in my bed that was obvious when I turned over and didn't float, but thumped. My daughter also tested my motherly love by keeping her thermostat at the usual setting of low, low, low. She could not survive in any type of heat. Fortunately, I knew that she liked living in arctic tundra conditions. To avoid frostbite I remembered to pack my thermal underwear.

A professional trucker, employed to drive the van back for us, flew in from Chattanooga to supervise the hired hands loading the moving van. I learned a valuable lesson regarding rental vans. Unless you are very cautious, one can be at the mercy of the company.

When I arrived to pick up the prearranged rental van, the only vehicle left for me was an old manual shift truck—take it or leave it. It was not what I expected, but had to accept if we were to leave on time. Our experienced driver was willing to put it on the road, even though he had serious concerns regarding its reliability. It turned out that I could compare it to the storied vehicle in the tale of *The Little Engine That Could*. The truck seemed to chug along, "I think I can. I think I can. I think I can." On the way back to the apartment I saw thick black smoke billowing from the truck's exhaust pipe, causing all traffic around us to swerve or change lanes to avoid that antique laboring down the road.

At 4:30 a.m. the next day, dark and early, we arose to begin last minute packing and have breakfast. The team of two workers and our driver arrived around 8:00 a.m. and began what looked to us like a loading marathon. We could hardly finish our packing before they were loading the boxes onto the van. The guys definitely had eaten their Wheaties that morning. They loaded everything possible until the van could hold no more. The driver paid the workers, said goodbye to us, and took off in the rented truck.

Now it was time for us to get the cats settled for our car trip. My child was very inventive. She had fashioned a large cardboard box with a hinged top that she placed on the back seat of the car. It was just big enough for her three large cats and a small litter box. To get them into the contraption, Hara had to load the cats, one-by-one, into the box while I held the top down to prevent their escape. I am not sure if the cats were curious or just petrified, but I could see little eyes, noses, and paws poking out of the air holes. Obviously, the cats were not very happy and did all they could to try to get out. Until all of the felines were safely secured, I had to place my body on the top and hope I was more determined than they were. Finally all three were in the box sealed with a lot of strong tape.

The gerbils rode in the trunk of the car in a small habitat. At least they seemed to be happy. Picture this scene: a car top carrier loaded to capacity, a trunk filled with miscellaneous bags, two guitars, a gerbil-filled habitat, along with a backseat loaded with a box full of cats. Up front were two already exhausted females. We departed Raleigh with deep sighs of relief, ready to get going.

During a filling station stop for gas, my daughter checked the trunk. Then I heard Hara yell.

"Oh no!"

"What's wrong?"

"The gerbils aren't here."

"What? Let me help you look. They can't be too far away."

We luckily found them scurrying about the trunk and put them back in the habitat. We had lowered the wall between the back seat and trunk to allow for more trunk storage. The cats could have had an unscheduled afternoon snack, as the air holes in the cats' box were big enough for a curious gerbil to enter.

Our next challenge was to find a motel that would accept pets. The AAA guidebook was helpful. We found suitable accommodations around 7:00 p.m. and began the process of unloading everything, because we did not want to risk having any of our possessions vulnerable to theft. My daughter placed each cat in a pet tote, again one-by-one, and deposited it in the room, while I repeated my role of holding down the box top against the remaining cats' attempts to be free again.

It took at least six trips or more to empty the car. The sun was slowly sinking, and so were we. By the time we dragged in the luggage, another hour had passed. We deposited the gerbil habitat on top of the toilet tank next to the bathroom sink. After a late room service dinner, I decided to take a shower. I can honestly say that was the first time I had showered in a bathroom with peeping gerbils. It was a little unsettling. I was exhausted, but Hara assured me that the cats would sleep with her as they usually did. How wrong that was. Atlas, Eros, and Apollo interrupted my sleep by jumping on my bed, crawling all over me, and licking my face. Of course, my daughter slept soundly, unaware that her pets loved me more than I wanted.

The six-thirty alarm rang much too early. The breakfast buffet was in a dimly lit dining room with soft mood music wafting through our ears. "Honey, you look sleepy," I told Hara. "I am," she replied. "I think the music is making me drowsy." We agreed that if we did not finish eating quickly we would be compelled to go back to bed.

Now we had the task of pet loading for a second time except for one minor problem; we could find only two cats. My daughter frantically searched for the missing traveler to no avail.

"I can't find Eros."

"Do you want me to take another look?"

"Go ahead. I'm going to the car with the other two cats."

Trying to give a thorough room inspection, I found the errant Eros, the youngest of the felines, hiding under the bed. I yanked him out, stuffed him into the tote, and flung him into the travel box so we could be on our way. My daughter took the wheel. Maneuvering the car through the twisting and turning portion of Highway 75 reminded me of my first roller coaster ride at Six Flags Over Georgia. We were on the last leg of the trip and feeling rather satisfied with our progress thus far. I should have known better.

"Honey, I know you are tired, let's change places.

"Okay. I guess I didn't drink enough coffee this morning."

I took over the driving, looking forward to finally reaching our destination. Soon I noticed the erratic behavior of the various gauges on the dashboard. First, the cruise control became unstable. Then the temperature gauge seemed static. We stopped for gas hoping to find a mechanic to look under the hood. All we found was a gas pump and a tackle and bait shop next to a sleazy motel, with no mechanic in sight.

As we approached the next exit, the car went into meltdown. One-by-one the temperature gauge, odometer, and speedometer registered zero. Thoughts of WWII movies flashed through my head. I saw the hero fighter pilot watching his gauges fail before bailing out over enemy territory. I didn't bail. The car coasted the downhill ramp to the gas station. There we were, miles from our final destination with a dead battery and a car full of live animals.

I placed a phone call to our emergency road service from a pay telephone. The telephone was located quite a distance from the stalled automobile. I asked the customer service operator to hold while I got additional information. On my way back to the phone, I spied a man holding my phone receiver, trying to make his call. "Sir," I called, "You can't use that phone!" I think he got my message by the disapproving look on my face. As I advanced towards him, he moved to another telephone. Of course, he left me with a disconnected call. My second attempt to secure help was successful.

We knew we needed to let our family know what was happening and arrange a ride for my daughter and her *children*. Hara knew we couldn't keep them contained for much longer and she was becoming increasingly stressed.

The road service driver in a flatbed truck arrived and informed me, "Lady, you aren't going to find an auto repair shop open on a Saturday anywhere around here." Our only option was to take the car to Ringgold and wait to have the car repaired on Monday. The man loaded our car onto the truck. One of the car's rear windows would not close due to the loss of electrical power. The driver said, "I think the cat box could fly out that open window onto the road. I wouldn't leave them there." That was a scary possibility. We decided that the gerbils were better off staying with me. Actually, I really had little say in the decision, but was in no position to argue. Therefore, I dutifully climbed up to the truck's raised passenger seat and placed the two gerbils in their habitat on my lap. As we slowly pulled away, I smiled wistfully at my daughter, who was looking very forlorn sitting on the curb watching her cats and waiting for her ride to come.

As the driver and I made our way along the interstate, I contemplated the next step waiting for us, helping direct the unloading of my daughter's stuff and unpacking. Never in my wildest thoughts could I have conjured the scene that greeted us as the tow trucker, disabled automobile, and I approached the Ringgold apartment. All I could do was laugh and sit there with my mouth open as I watched the rental van being towed away. It had also died on the front lawn of the apartment.

It took Hara a little longer to arrive than I expected. She had waited a long time sitting on the curb while her delayed rescuer learned that his transportation was a goner and switched to another vehicle.

Could there be an automobile virus infecting transportation? We learned that the rental van had begun to fail about halfway from Raleigh to Ringgold. "I coasted along a number of dangerous curves," the driver told me. "I held my breath." I guess the van was the little engine that couldn't.

We entered the apartment knowing our next chore was to clear a path from room to room. There were boxes and furniture everywhere, but not where they were supposed to be. Her belongings had been hastily strewn into the apartment so that the rental van could be towed away. We needed the skills of explorers Lewis and Clark to maneuver from downstairs to upstairs. Later that week I raised the white flag; I had endured enough. We drove to my Atlanta home in the repaired car. Those two weeks of packing, losing pets, and dealing with transportation problems just reinforced the need for an unfailing sense of humor.

After silence, that which comes nearest to expressing the inexpressible is music.

Aldus Huxley
English writer

My daughter's musical poetry is a form of release and therapy. Most of her songs relate to what she feels:

As I reflect upon my life I wonder what I could have done.
I feel that I've been good at heart and given it to everyone.
My soul I have forsaken as piece by piece I've carved away.
Supposed friends and lovers take their slice and then they run.
I hardly ever crack a smile without a lot of effort.
The humor that I hear is made at someone else's cost.

There's got to be a map for me somewhere below the dirt
Cause right now I feel misdirected, torn apart and lost.
My world has made me want to hide; it's safe here in the dark.
The sun is calling out my name to see the light of day.
I look around at all the things God made for me to see.
They're disappearing every day, a sign of our society.

My yesterdays won't go away, they haunt my present life.
I need to put the past away and let my spirit shine.
Although my soul is not yet whole, it's healing every day.
I can't give any more away, it is not yours it's mine.

Chorus:
>I sometimes wonder where they are
>The people who are genuine.
>The world's become a take and take.
>A stab in the back, a sign of the time.

Another song gives meaning to her experiences:

>I wasn't meant to be pushed around
>I wasn't meant to be clowned around
>I wasn't meant to be on the ground on my knees

>Questions here, questions there
>Answers that aren't anywhere
>Searching for the reasons that things are

>I'm always asking why, why, why
>And sitting there I realize
>I've never stopped looking inside of me

Chorus:
>Look to the sky
>And see me fly

When a man despairs, he does not write; he commits suicide.

> George Monro Grant
> Canadian Minister

CHATTANOOGA, TENNESSEE

Due to poor air quality, I was no longer able to breathe properly in Atlanta. Therefore, I moved to Chattanooga in 2003. In July 2006, I left Erlanger Hospital in Chattanooga to recuperate from spine surgery. My younger daughter had come to stay with me before and after my hospitalization. I was doing well. Hara had visited me in the hospital and said she would call a list of friends and family for me, to let them know I was doing all right. Once I settled in, I called my friends. Hara had spoken to everyone on the list and, from what they later told us, she seemed in a good humor. We had invited her to come to my house for dinner; she declined.

The next day we didn't hear from Hara all morning and tried to reach her. "Sometimes she doesn't hear the telephone when she is at her computer. She listens to music on her headphones," I said.

Her sister tried calling again; there was no answer. I told her, "Hara could be sleeping late; she doesn't always hear the phone." As the hours passed, I began to be concerned. She had not called to check on my well-being. We tried to reach her by telephone again. Still there was no answer. Now we both were worried.

"I think you should go over there. I'll give you my key to her apartment," I said. "All right, I'll call you when I get there." Then Hara's sister called me on her cell phone.

"Mom, I can't get in. All of the blinds are drawn. I can't see the inside. I've knocked loudly on the door and windows. She isn't responding."

"I think you should go to the office to see if someone can help."

The apartment maintenance man came and removed the entrance door that Hara had blocked with a heavy television set, other furniture, and tape. Her bedroom door was also taped shut. With effort, they gained entrance and found Hara almost unconscious on her bed. Her sister called 911; the paramedics tried to get her to respond.

It appeared that Hara had consumed a large number of prescription pills, along with alcohol and ice cream the night before. The paramedics had to wrestle with her to secure Hara on the stretcher. She was conscious enough to be combative until they were able to transport her to the ambulance. The same hospital I had left the day before admitted Hara, where she remained in intensive care until she was responsive enough to be in a standard care room.

Even though I wasn't supposed to be in a car so soon after surgery, I called a friend to drive me to the hospital. I had to be with my daughter. It was difficult seeing her so unresponsive. I thought she knew I was there, but couldn't be certain. I came home and decided it was best to let her sister handle the situation.

Hara was sedated most of the time. When she was able to respond, she had no recollection of the events and could not understand why she was there. The nurses had to restrain her hands to the sides of the bed. "Let me go! Get me out of here!" she screamed. She hallucinated, "I saw Dad in the room." At one point, she was convinced that the sitter who was there to keep an eye on her was going to kill her.

It was not until the next day that we found a suicide note taped to Hara's kitchen table. My younger daughter and I had gone to check on Hara's cats. The note indicated that Hara had made her plans in advance. Her instructions were to cremate her remains. Then we were to spread her ashes into the water on a Sarasota beach in Florida, near the school she had attended. Hara had even drawn a map to help us locate that favorite spot.

I recalled that she and I laughed at a statement she had made to me a few weeks earlier. "Mom, I don't think I am going to make it to the end of my life." "Do you know how ridiculous that sounds?" I replied. Of course, we both knew what she meant. It seemed to me that her guardian angel was still watching over her.

After several days in a mental health care facility to which Hara had been transferred, she finally came to grips with what she had almost done to herself, gave her sister a big hug, and thanked her for the rescue. She said really did not want to die, but believed that at least one of the prescriptions she had been taking affected her enough to conclude that suicide was the only option to relieve her depression.

"I'm sorry; I won't do anything like that ever again," Hara told us. She had no serious side effects from the ordeal. We were so frightened that she would have brain damage. Today she still has neck and shoulder pain resulting from her moving the heavy television set and fighting the restraints she had to endure while in intensive care.

The basic fact is that all sentient beings, particularly human beings, want happiness and do not want pain and suffering.

14th Dalai Lama/Tenzin Gyatso
Spiritual leader/author

Living with mental illness is similar to attempting to climb Mt. Everest every day of your life, and is no less daunting. My daughter's challenge is to get out of bed and summon the energy to gird herself with the stamina necessary to get through the day. She ingests multiple prescriptions to help her feel optimistic enough to complete the routine of the day. Some days the air is too thin, the struggle too difficult, and she waits until she feels more able to start the daily climb. Other days she finds it impossible to leave camp; her internal stormy weather is the barrier to a safe assent.

On the days when Hara thinks she will be able to get going, she may have to return, regroup, and try another day. Her Mt. Everest summit is feeling normal and being able to handle everyday stresses. She has told me that she doubts she will ever reach her peak.

The high cost of prescriptions presents another obstacle. We are grateful that she has qualified for Social Security Disability/Medicare and has some coverage from her former employer's insurance plan. Many homeless individuals are mentally impaired, but unable to afford the expense of life-altering medications. This could be happening to a friend, a co-worker, or a passer-by on the street. While in North Carolina, Hara had to file for bankruptcy. Her medical expenses exceeded her ability to pay. Her case is quite typical and very stressful. The financial challenge is constant, an endless struggle.

Hara filed for bankruptcy again years later. There is never enough money to pay for all the prescriptions, co-payments for the regular therapy sessions, and everyday living expenses. Hara now lives in a subsidized apartment for low income tenants in Chattanooga and knows she will never have her own home or a normal life—a dream unfulfilled.

Chattanooga, Tennessee

It is 2014. I live five minutes from Hara's apartment, and am thankful each day for her survival. She is still struggling, but trying to take better care of herself. My daughter began to perform her music again, to share her soul through her guitar, and has returned to painting. Hara is having difficulty remembering her melodies and lyrics, yet she perseveres.

One day we may be enjoying being together, laughing at jokes, playing the Rummikub game, and sharing a meal; the next, she is in despair that she has so many daily challenges. As she ages, other health problems afflict her. Currently Hara is receiving treatment with a psychologist and psychiatrist who are helping her cope with daily challenges. Her current prescription cocktail is working.

I am acutely aware that statistics reveal that individuals with mental illness have a shorter lifespan than the general population. Therefore, I cherish the days I spend with Hara, even when there are tears. I know she is still fighting the terrible illness; that is cause for hope. In her apartment is a favorite piece of art, a Peter Max print featuring W.C. Fields in the center. Could this be in fond recollection of her dad? She says it is, in spite of all that has happened.

Trying to understand you is like trying to smell the color 9.

Author unknown

Mental illness, misunderstood even today, is devastating for the sufferer. Left untreated, it is like a thief who slowly robs the victim of the essence of spirit and beauty of soul, leaving only suffering, anger, heartbreak, and often death. All who loved Paul are also victims. It has been many years since he died at the age of fifty-four. I called him mercurial, that his moods shifted from up and down like a thermometer. Perhaps a better analogy would be Dr. Jekyll and Mr. Hyde. As the years passed, the demarcation between the two became more pronounced. It never occurred to me that it was more than his personality quirk, which was primarily loving and giving. Was Paul the incurable romantic who in 1959, wrote the following to me?

"I miss you very much my darling. My heart aches when you are not near. The memory of your warmth keeps me going when we are apart. I think of all the good times we have had together. Even the sad times have great meaning to me. I am now, finally, a man because I have a woman such as you. We will have a long happy life together. Our love will grow and mature and envelope us in its comfort. God bless you for being you and for being mine."

Was this man the caring individual who insisted that my parents move into our home when they became too frail to care for themselves, so the family could be together? Or was he the angry person who fitfully threw an ashtray across the room and at a peak of distress stormed out of the house, not returning until mid-morning the next day? The answer is yes to all of the above.

When I recall the confusion I felt when Paul would go from expressing love, to finding fault, and showing anger toward me, I did not know that an individual with BPD might switch quickly from idealizing to devaluing caregivers. They expect that the other person will be there to meet their needs on demand. Just as Paul often had unrealistic beliefs in his own coping skills and denied anything was wrong, a symptom of many people who exhibit bipolar behavior, I was also one with unrealistic beliefs. I continued to convince myself that Paul was capable of responsibly controlling our finances. I believed that I was managing to keep our family intact. Neither was true.

Because Paul's existence wasn't always easy, he used humor to hide his suffering. My daughters and I laugh together, recalling their dad's habit of making silly faces or clowning around on his birthday with a large gift bow on his head. When they were young, the girls loved his way of twisting words to get their giggles going, such as saying Picknoso (Picasso) or Van Goo (Van Gogh).

Like her dad, Hara has a wonderful sense of humor and an unbridled determination to forge ahead, even when sidelined with depression. Both of my girls, now lovely women, have inspired me to continue to recognize humor in life's most challenging moments. I read a newspaper article written about a former prisoner of war who survived the Bataan Death March of World War II because, as he related, "I never gave up hope or lost my sense of humor." Like the soldier, finding reasons to laugh has been my salvation in times of stress and loneliness.

Not in the clamor of the crowded street,
Not in the shouts and plaudits of the throng,
But in ourselves are triumph and defeat.

H.W. Longfellow
Educator/poet

In the days of my youth in the 40s and 50s, mental illness happened to other people's families, not mine. A prevalent philosophy regarding delicate issues in my immediate family was, if you don't discuss it, it's not a problem. Humor wasn't my only coping mechanism. I probably had the cleanest house in Mobile, even in Alabama. I cannot claim the world cleaning championship, which belongs to my late mother-in-law. She told me in her early years she cleaned her bedsprings with a toothbrush and put newspapers over her newly mopped floors. Perhaps she, too, was attempting to cope with situations out of her control.

I do know I drove my daughters wild, particularly Hara. She would escape to her bedroom and listen to music on her headphones. When her sister had enough of my top sergeant inspections, she would leave to be with friends. I now confess the white glove dusting test was a little extreme. Trying to be super mom, super housekeeper, super everything did more to alienate my loved ones than I certainly intended. Maintaining my home was the only part of my personal life over which I felt I had command.

I have wondered if I had understood at the beginning of my relationship with Paul what I now know, could our lives have taken different paths? Probably. If I had recognized earlier what was really happening to my husband, would I have been better able to help him, myself, and later, our daughter? Definitely.

There is a story/legend dating probably as far back as 1500-1800 years, retold by a family friend, Rabbi Rick Sherwin of Congregation Beth Am in Longwood, Florida.

"There was once a queen who would leave her palace one day a week and walk toward the woods. At a certain spot, she told her attendant to wait for her, and she disappeared among the trees for about an hour. After several months, the curious attendant wanted to know where she went. She secretly followed the queen and saw her go into a small, dilapidated hut. Inside the structure was a box of old, torn clothes, and a mirror. The queen changed into these clothes and stood before the mirror. After a short time, she changed back into her queenly raiment and returned from the woods.

One week, the attendant could no longer contain her curiosity and, admitting that she followed the queen, asked directly: 'What is the structure? Why do you stand in front of the mirror dressed in tattered clothes?' The queen smiled. 'When I was a child, my family was very poor. By standing in the hut in front of the mirror I remind myself that life was not always what it is now. I emerge from the experience strengthened along with those who share that memory with me, and I appreciate life itself all the more.'"

This book is my mirror. As I reflect on what once were our lives, I realize I had been physically, emotionally, and spiritually dependent. I am grateful that I have survived with my sense of humor intact, and certain that I can live each day with deep appreciation for my wonderful daughters, son-in-law, grandsons, extended family, and treasured friends. I now sadly, but lovingly, recall when Pinny wrote to Snuffy:

". . . Each year becomes more rewarding and fulfilling when we are together, perhaps not physically, but at least in each other's thoughts. I'm sure we are blessed with many more wonderful years ahead and when we have had our share we will have a storehouse of wonderful memories to muse over."

It has been over twenty-eight years since Paul's death. Not only has his plant survived, it recently bloomed —the first time in over 20 years—it survived and so will we.

I believe that . . . hope always triumphs over experience—laughter is the cure for grief—love is stronger than death.

Robert Fulghum
Author

Epilogue

Help is available for depressed individuals. I encourage anyone who feels suicidal to seek professional help immediately. Families or friends of someone in this condition should do all they can to get the person to a mental health facility as soon as possible. The decision is not easy. Life can be better with treatment.

First the troubled person must acknowledge there is a problem and be willing to do whatever is necessary to begin treatment. Finding the appropriate psychologist and psychiatrist is a next step. Psychologists are trained therapists with a PhD, PsyD, EdD, or a master's degree in psychology. Psychiatrists are medical doctors who specialize in psychiatry. A primary care provider can be helpful in directing a patient to the appropriate psychiatric professional.

According to the Substance Abuse and Mental Health Services Administration, young adults with deep depression are more likely to use illicit drugs, start smoking, as well as abuse alcohol and pain medication than their peers. This fact has prompted many colleges and universities to prohibit on campus drinking. As we all know, that hasn't curbed alcohol abuse by students. The current statistics are staggering. I recently read reports of students who have died from alcohol poisoning. I can't recall that occurring during my college years. My conclusion is that abuse of alcohol is increasing; the solution to the problem eludes us. Until leaders understand the underlying reason why students feel the need/urge to consume unreasonable amounts of alcohol and tackle the problem as a mental health issue, I believe little will change.

National Resources

U.S. Department of Health and Human Services
Substance Abuse and Mental Health Services Administration
Center for Mental Health Services
P.O. Box 2345
Rockville, MD 20857
www.samhsa.gov

Suicide Hotline
1-800-784-2433
Adolescent Suicide Hotline
1-800-621-4000
Crises Intervention and Information
1-800-809-9957

National Alliance for the Mentally Ill
3803 N. Fairfax Drive
Suite 100
Arlington, VA 22203
www.nami.org

Mental Health America (formerly known as The National Mental Health Association)
2000 North Beauregard Street
Sixth Floor
Alexandria, VA 22311
www.mentalhealthamerica.net

Laying the Foundation- James J. Messina, PhD
Introduction to Laying the Foundation:
    The Dysfunctional Family Illness
    The Dysfunctional Family
    Looking-Good Behavior Characteristics
    Acting-Out Behavior Characteristics
    Pulling-In Behavior Characteristics
    Entertaining Behavior Characteristics
    Troubled-Person Behavior Characteristics
    Enabling Behavior Characteristics
    Rescuing Behavior Characteristics
    People Pleasing Behavior Characteristics
    Non-Feeling Behavior Characteristics
    Changing Old Behavioral Scripts

www.coping.us/layingthefoundation/familyselfesteemissues.html

RESOURCES FOR RESIDENTS OF TENNESSEE

Department of Mental Health and Substance Abuse Services
www.state.tn.us/mental/

Crisis Intervention and Information
1-855-274-7471

Suicide Hotline
1-800-273-8255

LOCAL RESOURCES FOR RESIDENTS OF GEORGIA

National Alliance on Mental Illness, Georgia
www.namiga.org

Georgia Crises and Access Line
1-800-715-4225

Lookout Mountain Community Services in Georgia
706-866-6885

NAMI Georgia
1-800-728-1052

Social Services Help Line
404-657-2273

LOCAL RESOURCES FOR RESIDENTS OF CHATTANOOGA

National Alliance on Mental Illness, Chattanooga
www.namichattanooga.org

Local Crises Intervention and Information
1-855-274-7471

Police
911 (ask for "Crises Intervention Team/CIT)

Helen Ross McNabb Center
423-266-6751
Hotline: 1-865-539-2409

Johnson Mental Health Center
423-634-8884
Hotline: 1-877-567-6051

Lighthouse Peer Support Center
423-756-1295

Moccasin Bend Mental Health Institute
423-265-2271

Parkridge Valley Hospital
423-499-2300

Made in the USA
Charleston, SC
07 July 2015